50
GREAT
CURRIES
OF INDIA

Camellia Panjabi was born in Bombay. She read Economics at Cambridge
and went on to become the Marketing Director of India's most prestigious
hotel group - Taj Hotels - known for spearheading new cuisines and culinary
ideas in its Indian, Asian and Western restaurants.

She has had a lifelong passion for food and for exploring different cuisines.
Over the last twenty years she has travelled the length and breadth of India
and has been involved in the setting up of several restaurants in these premier
hotels, featuring little known Indian dishes.

In 1982 she set up the Bombay Brasserie in London for the Taj Group, which
first introduced regional Indian cooking to the UK. In 1992 the restaurant
served its millionth customer.

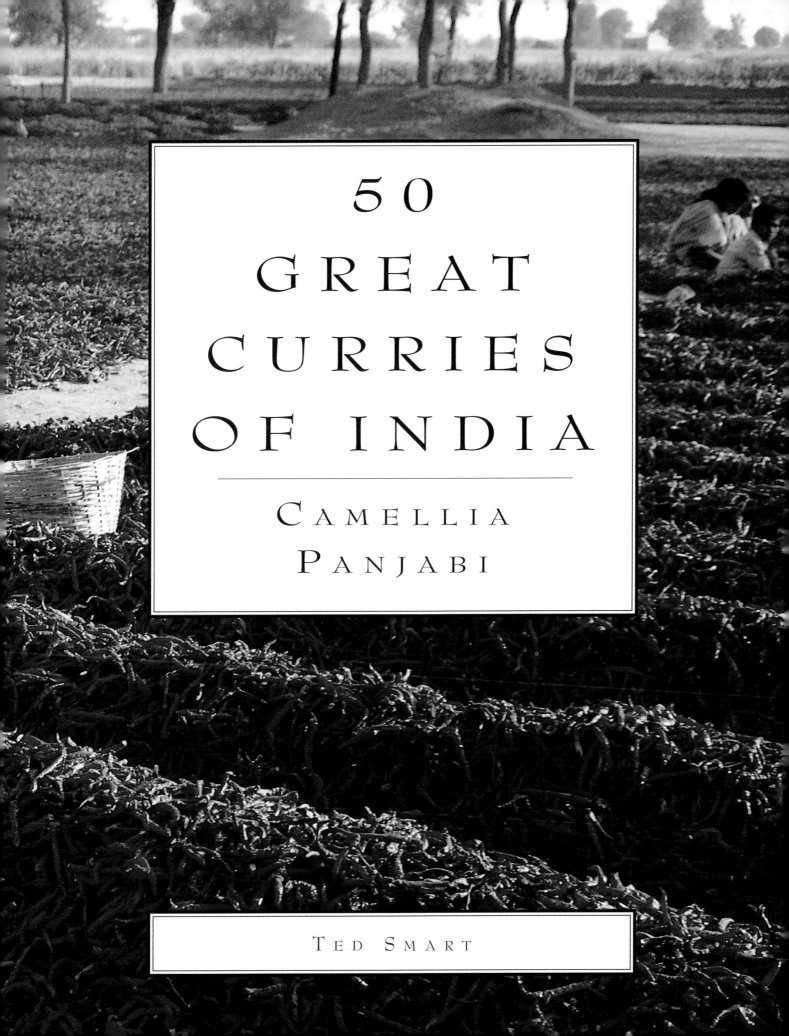

50

GREAT
CURRIES
OF INDIA

CAMELLIA
PANJABI

TED SMART

Screwpine flower

CONTENTS

This book is dedicated to the hope that the delicacy, depth and diversity of the cuisines of India may be better understood and appreciated in India and the rest of the world.

This edition produced for The Book People Ltd,
Hall Wood Avenue, Haydock, St Helens WA11 9UL

First published 1994 by Kyle Cathie Limited

First published in paperback 1995
Reprinted seven times

ISBN 1 85613 796 1

Hardcover edition published 1994.
Reprinted 1994 (twice), 1995, 1996, 1997, 1998, 2000 (twice)

A Cataloguing in Publication record for this title is
available form the British Library.

Design and typesetting by Geoff Hayes
Typed by Rollo Book Services Limited
Printed and bound in Singapore by Tien Wah Press

Photographic acknowledgements:

Those taken by Peter Knab, styled by Diana Knab and with
food preparation by Caroline Liddell, appear on pages
26, 29, 31, 35, 41, 43, 45, 47, 48, 49, 55, 56, 58, 62, 65, 66,
69, 70, 73, 74, 77, 78, 80, 83, 85, 87, 89, 90, 92, 95, 96, 98,
100, 102, 105, 107, 110, 114, 130, 135, 173, 178, 179

Those taken by Simon Smith, styled by Felicity Salter and with
food preparation by Kathy Man, appear on pages
36, 60, 112, 117, 118, 120, 123, 132, 136, 139, 140, 142,
143, 144, 147, 149, 151, 154, 158, 162, 167, 169, 170, 171,
174, 177, 181, 183

Ashvin Mehta took the photographs on pages 2–3, 19, 28,
44; Ashvin Gatha took those on pages 4 and 52–3; India
Photographic Co Ltd that on page 39 and Viren Desai those
on pages 1, 8, 12, 17, 23, 32, 42

The publishers wish to thank Thomas Goode & Co.
(London) Ltd for the loan of some of the china for the
photographs in this book.

ACKNOWLEDGEMENTS

My special thanks to: my sister, Namita, whose constant talk about curries got me started on this book; the Chairman of the Taj Group of Hotels, Ajit Kerkar, who has been my colleague for twenty-five years, and has always encouraged my curiosity and interest in good food, including travelling around India and overseas to discover it, the many chefs and colleagues in the Taj over this period with whom I discussed the many nuances of Indian food; the Taj as an institution for the opportunities it gave me to work on the setting up of restaurants all over India, London and Paris, and the travels all over the world which have enabled me to observe culinary influences around the globe and the difficulties that different nationalities have in understanding and appreciating Indian food.

To my mother, who from childhood has answered my incessant questions and brought to my attention so many insights on the health aspects of food. And to our cook at home, Rama, with whose help I was able to do all the permutations and combinations of recipes over the years.

My deepest thanks to Neville Abraham, who took great pains to write the notes on wine to go with Indian food and the particular wines to go with each curry. He has done a lot of experimentation and searching for the appropriate wines from all over the world to complement Indian food for the last few years, as he does the wine list for the award-winning Chutney Mary restaurant in London. Born in India, Neville founded the ground-breaking *Les Amis du Vin* wine company in London, and now heads a successful restaurant company.

I would also like to express my thanks to the following people who demonstrated their special recipes to me – Mrs Bashir, Roshan Tamboowala, Rehmatibal, Kusum Sahni and Shakuntala Kumari of Bissau, Taral Lalbhai, Umn Abdulla, Rekha Khanolkar, Varsha Mody and cook Babu.

To Kyle Cathie, my publisher, and Mike Shaw who so quickly showed a faith in the possibilities of this book. To Caroline Liddell who gave me many useful suggestions. To Helen Dore who diligently edited my manuscript.

And to the many friends who have opened up their kitchens to me, helping me to gain an insight into the finer aspects of the Indian home cooking in so many regions of the country.

NOTE

Cup measurements: In the recipes, the cup used to measure liquids – water, oil, yoghurt, etc. – is the equivalent of 7 fl oz (200 ml). The cup is also used as a convenient measure for larger quantities of herbs, such as coriander leaves.

Cooking times: It is hard to be precise about cooking times when preparing Indian food, as these depend to a great extent on size and cut of the pieces or meat, poultry and fish, and on whether these ingredients are on or off the bone. It is important to check carefully that everything is cooked to your satisfaction.

If you have any difficulty finding any of the ingredients in this book, contact the Curry Club, PO Box 7, Haslemere, Surrey GU27 1EP.

INTRODUCTION

Ever since I can remember I have loved and been passionately involved in food. From the age of five I wanted to be consulted at home on the menu that my mother discussed with the cook every evening for the following day. Lunch at school (Queen Mary's in Bombay) arrived from home in a tiffin-carrier, as it did for everyone else, and a large, warehouse-like hall with four long rows of benches housed the 300-plus girls who mouthed their way through lovingly cooked meals from home, brought by *ayahs* and drivers. I often walked between the benches eyeing the plates, taking in the colour, texture and aroma of everyone's lunch, which always seemed more interesting than my own. Then in the evening I would explain to my mother in great detail what the dishes that I coveted looked like, and entreat her to make them for me. As I grew older I began to tell her the names of the recipients, hoping she would recognize the communities they belonged to, and hence the dishes that I was raving about. But knowledge of the cuisine of communities other than one's own was very limited in those days. Strangely, it is only recently that I managed to track down the particular favourite (appearance-wise at least) of my childhood memories: a bright golden sunset-coloured curry that a Parsee girl sitting behind me often ate; known simply as 'fish curry' to the Parsees, this was a homestyle dish, never encountered since in any cookbook, or at dinner parties in Parsee homes, in restaurants or even at the famous Parsee wedding and *navjote* (thread ceremony) feasts.

A few years later, due to domestic reasons, my sister Namita and I signed up for 'school lunch', cooked and provided in a separate dining room for those children whose parents could not arrange for delivery of lunch to the school every midday. Our meal now consisted of 'English food' (Queen Mary's was run by Scottish missionaries): baked fish, baked mince (cottage pie), *dhol* (English and Anglo-Indian for lentil *dal*) and yellow rice, mutton curry and rice, coconut pancakes, and Malabar sago pudding, the taste of which I had never encountered before. Later I

A tiffin carrier

searched for years for the exact replica of the mutton curry – once, in the mid-sixties, I found it accidentally on the buffet table of the old-world West End Hotel in Bangalore, only to return in the seventies to find that the cooks of the old brigade had retired, leaving no recipes.

When I went to university in England, I was astonished to find at college dinner that the dishes had none of the spices and seasonings that we had experienced as children in 'English food' in India. It was then that I realized that 'Indian English food' was a sort of hybrid-cuisine in its own right, and was fairly widespread, being popularly eaten in India in clubs, where masala liver on toast was a favourite, on the railways which had to cater for British and Indian tastes alike, with the cooking done in cramped conditions by local cooks, and in *dak* government bungalows where masala omelette must have been and still is the number one seller, as well as popular restaurants like Gourdon and the Wayside Inn in Bombay, Koshy's in Bangalore and Flury's in Calcutta where cutlets were staple fare. (Incidentally, in India cutlets are patties made of a mash of anything – meat, fish, vegetables or chicken.)

As luck would have it, after a few years of marketing consumer goods in India, I landed in the hotel industry as the Sales Manager of the Taj Mahal Hotel in Bombay, a legendary hostelry about to embark on a once-in-a-lifetime renovation-cum-expansion programme to double its size and add an array of restaurants and banqueting facilities. The hotel already had a fine restaurant which can be best described as 'Indian French', a grand ballroom where a buffet lunch was served daily, and a bar and a grill. Next door was a sister hotel, the Greens, in the courtyard of which was an Indian restaurant known as Gulmohur, which served among other things the favourite Bombay dish, then newly discovered – Tandoori chicken!

In the mid-sixties my first mission was to increase the sales of this restaurant, where lunch-time business often consisted of six guests in an eighty-cover restaurant, with dinner for about twenty or thirty people who wanted only to sit in the courtyard and eat Tandoori chicken and *naan* bread.

There was no more than a handful of Indian restaurants in town at the time – Gaylord, Kwality's and Khyber. Gaylord's served Indian (meaning Punjabi), Continental (meaning Indianized English) and Chinese food and still remains one of Bombay's favourites; Kwality's and Khyber served Punjabi food with favourites like *tandooris*, butter chicken and *choles* (chickpeas). Apart from the Gulmohur at the Greens Hotel, none of the other hotels in town, primarily the Ritz and the Ambassador, had Indian restaurants. It just was not fashionable to eat Indian food in the mid-sixties to early seventies.

Inter-Continental hotels, who were advising us at the Taj on designing the range of restaurants to be included in the enlarged hotel, cautioned us not to plan for a total of more than three, but our heady young team wanted one of each – classical Indian, real Chinese, contemporary French, a casual eatery, a discotheque. We wanted everything the city never had. And we got it.

It is indicative of the time, though, that when conceptualizing the Indian restaurant, the interior designer (a Swiss living in Hong Kong and famed for his work on hotel interiors) decided he wanted to design the restaurant on the lines of a traditional South Indian temple with majestic carved pillars and a marble embellished dance-floor for classical South Indian dances to be performed every night. He wanted a grand brass oil-lamp to be placed at the entrance to the restaurant, for which the name suggested was 'Tanjore', after the town in which the most beautiful temples of South India are located – and which has now been declared a world heritage site by UNESCO.

Some of us muttered that we did not know much about the food of the region and that anyway the food of Tanjore was more likely to be simple Brahmin vegetarian, and as such not to our guests' tastes. Believing that the food of the restaurant need not be related to the name or the ambience, the Tanjore lobby won, and the restaurant stands to this day. It was the turning point in the restaurant life of India, however, making it fashionable to go out and eat Indian food in an elegant atmosphere. Perhaps the most popular Indian restaurant ever, its 120 seats have been occupied more than once every night for over twenty-two years. While the dishes change every few months, and now incorporate a few dishes from Chettinad in Southern India, the old favourites – the inevitable tandooris, kebabs and North Indian dishes – still dominate the menu. This leads us to the interesting question – when, where and how does interest in the regional cuisine of a country begin among its own people?

Over the ensuing years, I worked closely with a team of Taj colleagues opening hotels and new restaurants within the hotels in Madras, Goa, Delhi, Bangalore, Hyderabad and elsewhere. Interestingly, attempts to introduce regional Indian dishes in various menus always met with consumer resistance, in the sense that customers continued to order mainly the Punjabi dishes on a menu. In India, the majority of those who eat out as part of their lifestyle are Punjabis from the state of 20 million people in the north-west of India. They grow most of India's wheat and love their *naans* and *paratha* smothered in real *ghee* or butter, and their favourite dish is butter chicken – pieces of Tandoori chicken with tomato and butter sauce. Punjabis are the most outgoing of all Indians; they relocate themselves as corporate executives throughout the sub-continent, and when they go out they basically eat their own food, wherever they are. Since they form the backbone of the clientele of almost every Indian restaurant in the country, restaurant owners are wary about directing the menu away from Punjabi favourites. Also, city-dwellers in India somehow feel that since they can make the local cuisine at home, why spend money on this in restaurants; when people eat out, their two favourite choices are Punjabi and Chinese!

This is the main reason why regional Indian food has not come of age, even in India itself. Restaurateurs are wary of setting up restaurants specializing in cuisines other than North Indian. Calcutta, for example, has no well-known Bengali restaurant, while the most popular restaurant in the city, Amber, serves Punjabi food to hundreds of customers every day.

It was to combat this despairing feeling that one would never be able to present regional Indian food other than Punjabi cuisine to a restaurant-going public in India that led me to believe that perhaps it would be possible to launch a regional Indian cuisine in England, where acceptance of Indian food is high and regional cuisines of all kinds were being launched. To test the water, I thought what better way to start than with the food of my own city? And so the idea for what was later to become The Bombay Brasserie was born, although the notion that Bombay had a cuisine that would interest the outside world seemed to be fanciful beyond words.

This disbelief was shared not only among colleagues but also by professionals in the UK. A leading PR agency refused to handle our account unless I agreed to drop the name 'Bombay' from the restaurant name, saying their research showed the name was synonymous with squalor! There was immense pressure to do the usual thing – North Indian food, presented ethnic-style, with all the dishes presented simultaneously in nice metal bowls, with part-silver service as would befit the launch of a Taj restaurant in the UK.

I spent a few months in London in 1981, visiting every Indian, Pakistani and Bangladeshi restaurant of repute, going to the markets, talking to a great many foodies, chefs of all cuisines and restaurant owners, and built up a picture of different influences and consumer ideas about eating in restaurants at the time. Then I returned to Bombay to locate the kind of dishes that would fit in with what I had discovered. We took chefs out of regular hotel routine and for several months worked at homestyle recipes from the communities of Bombay. And so the menu for The Bombay Brasserie evolved.

Everything else developed logically out of this. To eat a number of items simultaneously on a plate meant larger plates were needed, and larger glasses, larger tables and so on were required. We were finally able to bring to London a mixture of homestyle Bombay dishes such as fish with green chutney baked in a banana leaf, the streetside food, the *sev batata puri* as well as the imperative North Indian favourites like Tandoori chicken, but extending the form of cooking to local ingredients like trout.

The Bombay Brasserie celebrated its tenth anniversary in December 1992, and over the years has given Indian cuisine a new perspective internationally. But even so, it was not followed by a string of successful regional Indian restaurants in the UK. Even in India there still remains only a handful, some of them specializing in North Indian cuisine. Perhaps a greater understanding of regional Indian cuisines will result in more regional restaurants. I hope my book plays its own part in this.

I often hear my non-Indian friends say that the best Indian food is to be had in people's homes. This is true. But Indian food at home is completely different from Indian food as most of the world knows it. In fact what most Indians know of food **other than their own** is restricted to what they eat in restaurants. Ninety-nine per cent of Indians do not have a *tandoor* and so neither Tandoori chicken nor *naan* is part of India's middle-class cuisine! This is so even in the Punjab, although some villages have communal *tandoors* where *rotis* (griddle bread) can be baked. Ninety-five per cent of Indians don't know what a *vindaloo, jhal farezi* or, for that matter, a Madras curry is. This is Indian food as eaten in Indian restaurants outside India.

Indians coming from different regions, religions and castes do of course share a common ethos with each other's cuisine in a limited way, a similar method of slow-cooking, and a commonality of food materials, particularly spices. They know their own cuisine well because, with the women of the house either doing or supervising the cooking, traditions continue. But their only knowledge of other cuisines is usually limited to those communities where they have friends and visit their homes for a meal. In any city in India there are several communities, including religions and caste communities. At weddings where guests run into hundreds, cooking is done by special wedding caterers and each community has its own. And this sector is a repository of culinary secrets as much as in homes where cuisine is taken seriously.

In the quest for excellence in making well-known dishes, I began to look everywhere over the last few years: an outstanding dish in a lowly eating house off a bazaar, a flavourful dish in an aristocrat's house in Madras, a crustacean curry at the table of Bombay's top society hostess, a great dish at the table of a gourmet family in Hyderabad, a third-generation wedding cook from Lucknow. Sometimes it meant piecing together different little secrets from several sources – for example, a hint from one master cook combined with hints from two Goan lady friends, to arrive at the best in the case of the Goa curry . . . and so a collection of recipes began to build up, extending from one file to several.

Then a couple of years ago, my sister Namita and some of her friends, opened a restaurant in London featuring Indian and Anglo-Indian cuisine, known as 'Chutney Mary'. The menu was a

very interesting one with a great many 'new' dishes. Late one night she called me in Bombay. 'Camellia,' she said, 'the world here wants magical curries. Do you have any in your collection?'

The word 'magical' set me thinking. This was along the lines of the personal quest I had embarked on a few years before, to discover what exactly made one version of a traditional Indian dish so much better than the same dish made by someone else who was also a knowledgeable cook. It was a question that constantly exercised my mind as at the Taj we endeavoured to raise the standards of popular dishes to match the rising expectations of customers who wanted all the familiar dishes, but they expected the hotel restaurants to cook them so much better. I was not able to pinpoint how to make that happen. My quest was leading me to the discovery that in India catering college-trained chefs were being taught by teachers of whom very few had accessed the real treasure storehouse of Indian cuisine. This storehouse was diversified among the professional cooks who for generations had cooked for weddings and traditional banquets, the cooks who worked for families who took pride in their table, and quite a few housewives whose tables were legendary – those were all a class apart. And this was where gourmet Indian cuisine had been practised, apart from the older best hotels in each city which had in the early half of the century attracted the best Indian traditional cooks. These have mainly been replaced by a new generation of professionally trained chefs from catering colleges, of whom a few having learned from the 'magical' old hands in their kitchen have soared above the rest. But by and large the limited recipes taught in the colleges were percolating down to all hotel restaurants, both in India and overseas. So I began to look for recipes which were better than the run of the mill. This book is the result.

Those who cook and those who appreciate good Indian food are today desirous of knowing more about traditional regional Indian dishes. And curries are the fulcrum of an Indian meal. A better appreciation and understanding of the differing tastes of the many regional cuisines of India will also enable hoteliers and restaurateurs to have the confidence to put such items on their menus. An awareness of the dishes will enable the customer and the chef to travel the same path together. And the fact that many men and women in India and around the world will be able to enjoy these dishes in their own homes, in the company of those who would be happy to eat it, has spurred me on to write this book.

I am indebted to all those who helped me make this book happen: the many cooks, housewives, professional gourmets, those whose business it is to do party catering – all of those who shared their culinary secrets. It has not been possible for me to name all those who freely gave of their time and knowledge over the years, but to them I owe a great deal.

CULINARY INDIA

At different points in its history, India was influenced by many foreign cuisines as the result of invasions and rule by invaders. Another major influence on Indian cuisine, apart from these cultures in India, has been the ancient Hindu treatise on health, the Ayurveda, as well of course as the countless other traditions that an ancient civilization develops over the centuries. As Indians now relocate from one part of the country to another, and restaurateurs set up establishments in regions of India other than their own, cross-fertilization between the sub-cuisines of India is taking place. Enterprising Punjabi restaurant owners have taken Tandoori chicken, *naan*, butter chicken, *chole* and *tarka dal* throughout India and abroad, and Punjabi cooking has begun to influence homestyle cooking all over India. The caterers of Udipi (a village near Mangalore) have given all India and many parts of the globe a taste of *idli*, *dosa* and Madras coffee.

But many local Indian culinary practices are still little-known outside their regions. Political boundaries were drawn within the sub-continent after independence in 1947 and, today, although one may refer to the cuisine of a political state within India (based largely on language), the culinary boundaries do not necessarily coincide with the political ones.

As with all cuisines, the regional produce forms the base. The Malabar coast of Kerala, with its profusion of pepper and *garam masala* spices, uses these liberally in cooking, and most, though not all, Kerala food is spicy-hot. When it is not the case, the restraining hand of Brahminism has come into play, as spicy food is said to activate sensuality and consequently inhibit clear and high thinking. So the food of the Namboodri Brahmins is mild.

Thus, the influence of *religion* and *caste* is also important. Within Hinduism there are two main streams: the Vaishnavites and Shaivaites – the followers of the gods Vishnu and Shiva respectively. While the Brahmins in both communities are largely vegetarian, there is a much larger incidence of vegetarianism among the Vaishnavites. Other religions, like Jainism, which was a reformation movement among some Hindus, advocate a strict code of vegetarianism.

Geography itself has a part to play. Along some coastal regions of India, notably Bengal and in Maharashtra among the Saraswat Brahmins, fish is eaten by Brahmins without losing caste. Climate, income levels, traditions and beliefs all influence cuisine. So do the preferences of the palate which differ between communities. The food of the people of Nellore and Telangana (in Andhra), Chettinad (in Tamil Nadu) and the Syrian Christians (of Kerala) is fiery-hot. That of West Bengal is mild and sweet, while in East Bengal – now Bangladesh – it is much hotter, though the dishes in both Bengali cuisines are the same. The food of Gujarat is mildly spiced and sweetish – the people use *jaggery* in their cooking, even in savoury dishes – while in nearby Rajasthan, with its arid landscape, the food is more pronouncedly spicy.

As far as curries are concerned, the rice-growing regions of India have a large number of curries with thinner gravies specially meant for eating with rice, while curries in the wheat belts of India have thicker gravies well-suited to eating with *rotis* and *parathas*. In this book an attempt has been made to give a glimpse of most, though not all, the cuisines of India, outlining their distinguishable differences in taste. I hope you will be tempted to delve further.

AFGHANISTAN

PAKISTAN

Kashmir
red chillies
crocus

Himachal Pradesh
apples

Punjab
mustard

CHINA

INDUS

guavas

sugar cane

NEPAL

Rajasthan

coriander

goats

maize

Uttar Pradesh

rice

coriander seed

GANGES

TIBET

Sikkim

BHUTAN
BRAHMAPUT

Assam
tea

pineapples

Gujarat
groundnuts

cumin seeds

red chillies

NARMADA

Madhya Pradesh

Bihar

BANGLADESH

**West
Bengal**

onions
turmeric
oranges
limes
millet
lychees

Maharashtra

Orissa

keora flower

custard apples

BAY OF BENGAL

Andhra Pradesh

Goa —
mangoes
coconut

Karnataka
red chillies
grapes
coffee
tea

Tamil Nadu
coconut
turmeric

CAUVERY

I N D I A

Kerala —
coconut palms
cardamoms
pineapples
red bananas

INDIAN
OCEAN

THE PHILOSOPHY OF INDIAN CUISINE

When I mentioned that I was writing an Indian cookbook to the famous chef and cookery writer Anton Mosimann, he said, 'Do write about the philosophy of Indian cuisine. It's so difficult to cook something well without first understanding what the philosophy of the cuisine is.' Of course, he is right. But trying to explain the philosophy of an ancient and complex cuisine in simple terms is no easy task, because one cannot attempt to describe the significance of one set of factors without outlining how it connects to others. So I will try to identify the various elements that underlie the system of beliefs on which the philosophy of Indian cuisine is based.

India is of course a sub-continent, equal in size to Western Europe, but without a single common language. It has about two and a half times the number of people, several language scripts and many more religions. So it is not easy to label its cuisine under a single heading. One has to allow for differences in climate and availability of produce, and vast differences in income among the people, as well as different religions, customs, traditions and beliefs.

The strongest influence on Indian cuisine, or at least among 80 per cent of Indians – the Hindus – is Ayurveda, an ancient body of knowledge on health. *Ayur* is derived from the word *ayus* meaning span of life in Sanskrit, and *veda* means knowledge. Thus *Ayurveda* is the knowledge concerning the maintainance of long life. Its origins are in the *Atharvaveda*, the contents of which date from around 1000 BC. Then in 200 BC a medical treatise called *Charaka Samhita* was written in Sanskrit by a sage called Charaka, who re-edited *Agnivesa*, a text written earlier by a sage of the same name along with five others, outlining the science of prolonging life without illness. *Samhita* means compilation. It deals with the origin of medical science, a detailed classification of diseases, all food and drink substances and details of lines of treatment, the use of drugs, diet and practices for achieving good health. In all there are 150 chapters on specific topics.

Numerous other texts were composed through the centuries, and the Ayurvedic tradition continued as a vigorous and expanding scientific tradition up to the sixteenth century. Ayurvedic texts were translated into Greek by Cridos (300 BC), Tibetan and Chinese (AD 300), Persian (AD 700) and Arabic (AD 800).

Ayurveda is not confined to medicine only: it covers the whole subject of life in its various ramifications. It discusses the purpose of life, the importance of mental as well as physical health, and a code of ethical conduct for healthy living. The aim is salvation – to keep the body as well as possible and to give life such quality that one can progress beyond it. Life is a combination of the mind, body and soul, and this is in fact the central subject of Ayurveda.

'He alone can remain healthy, who regulates his diet, exercise and recreation, controls his sensual pleasures, who is generous, just, truthful and forgiving, and who gets along well with his relatives (i.e. enjoys a happy family life, in an extended sense).' It is amazing that all these observations were made thousands of years ago, while it is only in recent times that scientists and thinkers have observed that a lot of diseases emanate from bottled-up emotions, grief and negative thoughts.

Ayurveda understands the properties and actions of food differently from Western science. The bio-chemistry of an edible product is not everything. For example, vegetable oil and dairy fat, such

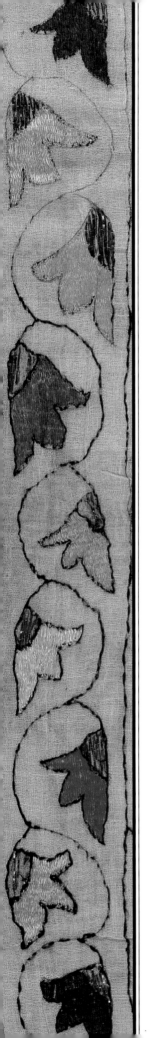

as *ghee* from cow's milk, are not seen merely as fats, but in terms of their effects on the body, which are supposedly very different. *Ghee* is cooling on the body while oil heats it. Another special quality of *ghee* is that it assimilates the good properties of the foods it is mixed with and adds them to its own, without losing any of its own properties, while oil undergoes a transformation when it assimilates the properties of other food.

According to Ayurveda, the human body is composed of seven body elements or tissue layers. These are plasma (sometimes called the 'skin'), blood, muscle, fat, bone, nerves and marrow and reproductive secretions. And there are innumerable channels that supply the various tissue constituents. Good health means proper flow through these channels and an equilibrium in the proportions of the seven body elements.

Also, there are three primary life-forces in the body, or three biological humours. The Ayurvedic term for humour is *dosha*, that which causes things to decay. The humours correspond primarily to the elements of air, fire and water, and in Sanskrit are called *vata, pitta* and *kapha. Vata*, translated as wind, means that which moves – for example, breathing and beating of the heart; *pitta* is fire, *dosha* translates as bile, that which digests things, including mental digestion, or the ability to comprehend reality; and *kapha* as phlegm, that which holds things together.

Ayurveda believes that when the humours are out of balance and aggravated they manifest symptoms and give rise to various diseases. The excess humours move into the body's channels, causing improprieties in their flow. Diseases should first be treated with food and medication only later if required. The treatments using foods are based on the six tastes (*rasa* in Sanskrit) – sweet, sour, salty, pungent, bitter and astringent. Each taste has its specific therapeutic actions. The tastes increase or decrease the biological humours, as the case may be. Everyone needs a certain amount of each of the six tastes, and relative proportions differ according to the constitutional or humour type of the particular individual. Too much of any one taste is harmful to any constitutional type.

The sweet taste gives strength to the tissue elements, is good for nourishment, and harmonizes the mind. Sweet-tasting products are not only those which taste sugary, but include rice, *ghee* and fruits. Sweet food is heavy on digestion, however.

The sour taste stimulates the digestive fire and enzymes and sour-tasting food, for example lime and tamarind, are easy on digestion and good for the heart. (It is only relatively recently that modern dietetics has decreed that vitamin C is good for the heart, and vitamin C is found in all sour foods!) By sour the Ayurveda means naturally so, not man-made sour items such as vinegar.

The salty taste stimulates digestion, clears obstruction in the channels in the body, causes sweating, and increases the power of digestion, but tends to deplete reproductive secretions. An excess of salt causes greying and wrinkling.

Pungent tastes, as in onion, pepper and garlic, help digestion, improve metabolism and dilate channels in the body. Foods with bitter taste eliminate bacterial elements, purify the blood and are light on digestion. Examples include bitter gourd, fenugreek seeds and lemon rind. Substances which have a predominance of astringent taste, such as betelnut leaf, most green vegetables and foods containing tannin like tea, possess the properties to heal ulcers and wounds. They dry up moisture and fat in the body and act as water-absorbents.

What I find most interesting is that the only other cuisines which give an important role to the sour, hot and astringent tastes are those of Thailand and Indo-China, where through maritime connections Hindu influences became assimilated. In fact the ancient capital of Siam was called

Ayuthya after Ayodhya, the capital of God-Hero Ram's kingdom in northern India, and the Angkor Wat temples have a Hindu influence. Galangal ginger (which has an astringent taste and features widely in Thai cuisine) is mentioned in ancient Ayurvedic texts as a medicinal plant.

A lack of any of the six tastes in the food will also aggravate the relevant humours. So now one can appreciate the raison d'être of the complexity of the Indian meal, which includes a spicy-sour taste mix, a yoghurt-based item, a dash of a hot and bitter pickle (often lime with the bitter rind), and a sweet. The traditional Indian *thali* meal (served in several small bowls on a large silver tray) has been devised to contain these complex requirements in a way that can be replicated every day.

A typical everyday meal: dal and rice, potato with greens, yoghurt,
raw onion, lime pickle and papad.

Ayurveda characterizes food and drugs in three :

1   Firstly, by its tastes (called *kasa* in Sanskrit, which, as explained above, act on different humours.

2   Secondly, by the potency (*veerya*) of the action it has on the body. All food items can be classified as either cold or hot on the body.

3   The third categorization is by way of special action on the body (*prabhava*). For example, two food or drug items may be similar in relation to their taste and potency but differ in their special action: for example, figs and dates are sweet and heatening, but figs have purgative qualities.

Equally, all human beings can be classified into three mental types. A person is made up not only of physical or bio-chemical elements, but also of non-apparent constituents. These constituents decide the responses to stimuli that are received by the individual. These differences are governed by the qualities of *Satva, Rajas* and *Tamas. Satva* means pure and therefore a person who has

dominant Satvic traits will be a thinker on a higher plane, will have more curiosity, strive hard for real knowledge and will try to win in competitive situations by adoption of fair means. A person who is Rajsic will be basically a doer, industrious and domineering, who will use almost any means to succeed. A Tamasic person will not even have a desire to learn or put in effort and lacks the intellectual capacity to encompass the gravities of a situation.

Different types of food can contribute a *Satva, Rajas* or *Tamas* influence. Food which is easily digestible, fresh and ripe, can be cooked by a simple and quick process (though not in a microwave oven!), the total quantity taken being of moderate quantity, contributes to strengthening of Satvic forces. The person consuming such food is alert, quick-thinking and in harmony with nature. He is stimulated by or quick to grasp even the slightest stimuli.

Highly spicy food, food produced by suppressive means (such as battery-produced eggs) or the meat of slaughtered animals is *Rajas*-dominant. The person who consumes such food loses the capacity to distinguish the more subtle stimuli and as time goes on requires stronger ones to reach a good level of deep understanding.

Food that has a preponderance of oily and spicy ingredients, and food that is overcooked, stale and unclean, is liked by people in the state of *Tamas* or ignorance. All 'junk' food would be included in this category, because it is basically prepared long before being eaten.

Ayurveda believes that sciences related to health and disease should make an attempt to study the omni-substances of behaviour, because the needs of different personality types differ. The constitution of the mind has a role in preserving health and diseases of the body.

A practitioner of Ayurveda, when prescribing a diet for a person, would take into consideration his disposition, body type (which humour dominates his constitution), the season (because the humours behave differently in different seasons and food has to be adjusted for their heating and cooling properties) and particular state of health. He would tend to advise eating foods that grow in the region in that season. That is nature's way of balancing the requirements of the body.

The Ayurvedic texts also describe the methods of foods preparation and consumption. Food should be prepared with love and good feeling. Hence even in affluent homes, in spite of having domestic help, many housewives cook for the family, though the help will prepare the food.

Food should be consumed in relative quietude, quite contrary to the Western emphasis on conviviality and conversation. Surprisingly, alcohol is not forbidden by Ayurveda. On the contrary, the *Charaka Samhita* lists eighty-four types of alcoholic preparation and claims that they strengthen the mind, body and the power of digestion, and help in overcoming sleeplessness and grief. Practical observations and remarkably relevant today, considering when they were written!

Similarly, meat or fish is not expressly discouraged. In fact the *Charaka Samhita* includes goat, chicken, antelope and turtle in those meats that are particularly good for health! However 'we are what we eat.' (*Upanishads*). Flesh has the force of violence in it, and the negative emotions of fear and hatred as part of it. It has therefore no place in a Satvic diet.

Generally, Ayurvedic teachings exhort people to follow a pure lifestyle, one that gives clarity and peace of mind. Physical purity involves a wholesome diet with emphasis on raw or freshly cooked vegetarian food, pure air and water, proper exercise of a calming nature (yoga) and physical cleanliness. Purity of mind involves non-violence, friendliness and compassion and a means of earning a living that does not bring harm to others and provides a service to humanity.

WHY AN INDIAN MEAL?

The world's eating preferences are becoming unified. First, it was the high-protein diet that won a following, then the white meat variation of the protein-dominated diet took over. Now the world is moving towards the Mediterranean diet, dominated by carbohydrates and flavoured with olive oil, tomatoes and basil. Thai cuisine, with its aromatic blend of herbs, chilli, ginger and lemon flavours is becoming increasingly popular.

Indian cuisine combines all of these characteristics. It is first and foremost carbohydrate-dominated, with emphasis on wheat *chapatis* and rice as a staple food. Everything else is in a sense an accompaniment – curry, as we shall see, is a flavoured dish to eat with Indian bread or rice. Unlike pasta, Indian *roti* is a wholewheat bread, retaining the entire goodness of the grain. Traditionally it was eaten with a dab of *ghee*, which is revered for its health-giving properties in India, but today uncooked oil is substituted. The rice that comes from the growing areas of the south is of the parboiled variety, partially boiled with the husk, then dried and milled, which retains more goodness than the polished variety.

Vegetables play a more dominant role in Indian cuisine than in perhaps any other. Usually one green and one other vegetable form part of every meal. India offers an array of vegetables unequalled anywhere in the world, and a variety of ways to cook each one.

Protein is also present in the Indian diet, of course, but much more effort is made to use protein derived from lentils and dairy products, rather than from meat. Legumes or *dals* boiled with herbs and tomatoes, seasoned with spices and eaten with rice, provide the amino-acid balance that constitutes 'complete protein'.

Meat and fish are eaten too, but in smaller quantities, well-spiced and flavoured to give satisfaction. It is a little-known fact that even when affluent Indians eat meat, it is in a very small quantity per meal – about 4oz (120g) of meat, poultry or fish on the bone. The composition of a meal would be about 2–3oz (60–90g) of actual flesh, a portion of vegetables, and maybe an additional root vegetable like potato, a pulse such as lentils, and a grain (wheat or rice), 2–3 tablespoons of *raita* (whisked and flavoured yoghurt), a little fresh herb chutney (for chlorophyl) and a *cachumber* of raw vegetables like onions and tomato.

The role of yoghurt (which should be live) is very important because it introduces good flora into the digestive system. A vegetarian meal inclines toward being alkaline which is much better for

health than an acidic one. But in India even a non-vegetarian meal is usually followed by fresh fruit which provides the alkaline balance.

As in Thai food, ginger, chilli and a sour accent are also essential, as are garlic and a range of spices. Spices play an important role in keeping the intestines decongested – they have an anti-inflammatory action as in the case of turmeric; anti-bacterial, as with curry leaves; digestive functions, as with cumin and clove; and anti-flatulent properties, as with asafoetida. Certain spices have particular actions – for example, coriander seeds have diuretic properties and black pepper dries mucus. The composite effect of a combination of spices is to facilitate digestion and ensure a cleaner intestine, which is believed to be the key to good health.

In terms of use of time, Indian food has certain specific advantages. First, many items can be cooked a day in advance. The dough for bread can be made a day ahead, as can lamb, chicken or fish curry which should be kept in a refrigerator: in fact curries taste better the following day. Lentils (*dal*) can also be made a day ahead, but should be freshly seasoned. Vegetables are best prepared just before they are to be eaten, as is yoghurt *raita*. Rice should also ideally be made fresh, though cooked rice can be eaten a day later.

What many Indian working women do nowadays is to make a fried onion, ginger, garlic, tomato and spice *masala* mixture (*daag*) and keep it in the refrigerator for up to two weeks, or longer in the freezer. Whenever they want to make a curry they heat a few spoonfuls of it with some oil, add the meat, chicken, fish or vegetables, and sauté for a few minutes, add some water and with no further effort they have a curry. Even when cooking a 'dry' vegetable, they put a few spoons of the mixture in a wok, with maybe just a quarter cup of water, then add the vegetables and cook over a low heat. It is a simple and effective method, especially useful for working women.

Indian food is also quite economical to prepare as expensive cuts of meat are not essential, and, as explained above, small quantities of meat combined with vegetables, lentils, yoghurt, rice and *chapatis*, make up a meal. With other additions such as chutneys, *cachumbers* and *papadams* a table for an Indian meal looks quite bountiful.

To make a *daag* curry base for storing in a refrigerator or freezer:

2lb (1kg) onions	*4 teaspoons coriander powder*
1½ x ½ in (4 x 1cm) piece of fresh ginger	*½ teaspoon cumin powder*
6 plump cloves garlic	*½ teaspoon turmeric powder*
3–4 green chillies	*½ teaspoon garam masala*
6 tomatoes (small)	*½ cup chopped coriander leaves (optional)*
½ cup oil	*1 teaspoon salt*

1 Chop the onions finely. Chop the ginger, garlic and chillies. Purée the tomatoes.

2 Heat the oil in a pan and fry the onions until dark brown (about 20–30 minutes). Add the ginger, garlic and chillies and continue frying for 3 minutes. Add the coriander powder and sauté for 4–5 minutes, stirring continuously, adding 2 tablespoons water if the mixture sticks to the bottom of the pan. Then add the cumin, turmeric and *garam masala*. After 30 seconds, add the tomato and coriander leaves. Stir, add 2 cups water and 1 teaspoon salt and cook over a low heat for 15 minutes.

3 Remove from the heat, allow to cool completely, then store in a jar in the refrigerator or freeze. For 1–1¼lb (500–625g) lamb, chicken, fish or vegetables, use one quarter of this mixture.

WHAT EXACTLY IS A CURRY?

Curry, as the word is used today in India, simply means gravy. In the West, gravy is a liquid sauce made with juice from the meat, and thickened with flour and seasonings. Indian curry or gravy is made by cooking the meat or vegetables along with lots of ingredients including thickening agents and a combination of spices but using no flour. Western dishes most closely resembling curry are ragoût, navarin and hotpot.

A lot has been written about the word curry and whether it is actually an Indian word in the first place, or was invented by the English. The Tamils (the people living in the Southern Indian state of which Madras is the capital) have the word *kaari* in their language, which has twelve vowels instead of the five in English and slightly different phonetic emphasis changes the meaning of a word. (*Kaari* is actually part of a longer word, *Kaikaari*, in the Tamil region, where caste differences are taken seriously, and these are reflected in different meanings of *kaari*.) The Brahmins of Tamil Nadu, who are strict vegetarians, mean by *kaari* a vegetable dish cooked with spices and a dash of coconut. When the non-vegetarian communities of Tamil Nadu use the word *kaari*, it literally means meat, which they pronounce with more emphasis on the end of the word as in *kaaree*. They would call a meat dish with gravy a *kaaree kolambu*, *kolambu* being gravy. **The origin of the word curry seems to be a meat or vegetable dish to be eaten with rice, which is considered to be the main dish of the meal.**

The English first established trading stations and factories (which in those days meant agencies) on the Cambay (west) coast of India in the early seventeenth century. But with Robert Clive's activities in Madras in the mid-eighteenth century, the English settlement there slowly grew into a thriving trading station, and much later women arrived from England and households were set up. Naturally, hiring of local cooks and servants followed. Hence certain regional dishes were borrowed and adapted – Tamil 'pepper water' was one of these, with *muloga* (pepper) and *tani* (water) making up the popular mulligatawny soup. Even today the Anglo-Indians of South India make a soup called pepper water. Madras curry became synonymous with a hot curry: later on when people who were fond of curries returned to England, the curry powder trade was established in Madras where it continues to this day.

Cooks in English households in Madras would not have been Brahmins, who would have refused to handle non-vegetarian food. They would most probably have been from the castes who converted to Christianity, who would agree to cook meat, beef and pork. So they would certainly have referred to meat dishes to go with rice as curry.

In Northern India, particularly Punjab, *khadi* means a gravy dish made out of powdered gram lentil and yoghurt which is often served with dumplings. Similarly, in Gujarati, the same word means a yoghurt-based gravy eaten with rice. To the Sindhis curry means a lentil dish made with *thur dal* and gram flour, served topped with a medley of vegetables as a popular Sunday lunch dish, eaten with rice and fried potatoes. To the Bori Muslim community of Bombay *kaari* is the Bori curry made with meat or chicken on a base of powdered peanuts and grams.

Curry means a dish with gravy, specially suited to combine with rice, and since it is widely believed that Indians always eat rice, does every meal include a curry?

In fact rice is not always part of a meal except in Southern India and Bengal and for the more affluent Gujaratis for whom rice follows the *poori* or *chapati* in a *thali*. The rest of India would have home-made *roti* made of millet or wheat, and only on some occasions would rice accompany *roti*, which would be eaten dipped in a *dal* or vegetable made not too dry as an alternative to a dish with gravy or curry. Similarly, rice is most commonly eaten with lentils, which would normally be accompanied by a vegetable. In affluent homes a dry meat or fish dish, such as a *bhuna*, might also be served with *dal* and rice, India's national dish, but this is not an everyday menu. The important point is that it is incorrect to think of rice and curry as inseparably linked.

A housewife choosing to include a curry when composing a menu, would do so in preference to a liquidy *dal* or a gravied yoghurt (*dahi khadi*) to accompany rice and/or *roti*. The rest of the vegetables being made would be dry. In such a situation she would make a semi-solid *dal* and would also choose to make a curry rather than a dry version of the meat so as to feed more people. Curry can be stretched even further if mutton or chicken, say, is combined with vegetables like potatoes, turnips or spinach. The curry has to complement the other dishes being served in terms of the quantity of gravy, colour, flavour and spiciness. If other dishes are brown or yellow, a green curry such as meat with spinach would be suitable. And if the curry is going to be a brown one, it would go well with a yellow *dal* and a green vegetable.

In a way Indian cuisine is like classical Indian music. It has been handed down through generations without a written code. So curries, like other dishes, have always lent themselves to improvisation.

Since there are no rigid or classic recipes for any curry dish – any number of good cooks would have a different recipe for the same dish – one really has to search for the best-tasting version of a particular dish. This is, of course, how this book came about. Choosing a good recipe for a dish is a subjective matter, and means that you are free to change the recipe to suit your taste. You will not be breaking any rules in doing so. This is the interesting point about Indian cuisine. In addition to its immense diversity, it offers a great deal of flexibility. So please mix and match to suit your taste, and increase or decrease your ingredients as you prefer . . . just so long as you can understand what each ingredient can do for you.

Let us now look at the basic principles of how to make a curry.

MAKING A CURRY

The starting point in making a curry is to **choose a cooking pot with a non reactive inner surface.** Most curries have a sour ingredient, so if a copper or brass pot were used it would have to have a tin lining. Stainless steel is better from the reactive point of view than aluminium or enamel but the pot should have a thick base or the spices will stick while frying. Traditionally in India, brass pots were used which were re-tinned regularly. In southern coastal India terracotta pots were and are still used, especially for making fish curries, as these have a strong sour tang. And as unglazed terracotta 'breathes' and allows aeration, fish curry can be kept for a while without refrigeration in a hot climate. For fish you need a wide but not very deep pot so that the pieces of fish can be laid flat without being one on top of the other. For a curry with lots of liquid a deeper pot is necessary. A flameproof casserole-type dish made of earthenware is ideal for making curries of all types, as are saucepans, particularly those with flared sides which make it easier to fry spices etc. Non-stick pots are suitable for Indian foods as onions and spices can be fried without sticking.

All curries have a main **ingredient** such as meat, fowl, eggs, or a single vegetable like potatoes, brinjals (aubergines), mushrooms, or a mixture of vegetables such as peas, diced carrots and french beans or potatoes and cauliflower.

Indian pots suitable for curry-making come in many shapes and sizes

Most curries start with the heating of cooking fat. Traditionally Indians prefer to use *ghee*, which is clarified butter, believing it to be more nutritious and to give better flavour to the food. *Ghee* does indeed give a wonderful flavour but nowadays most people use oil instead because of the cholesterol factor. In western India, groundnut oil is most popular, in parts of South India it is sesame oil, while in Kashmir and Bengal mustard oil is used; sunflower and corn oil are also becoming popular throughout the country. You can use the oil of your choice. Because spices and onions have to be fried for a while at the start of making a curry, butter is not suitable as it burns and turns brown very quickly. The amount of oil needed varies with the shape of the pan. If there is too much oil, refrigerate the curry and the oil will solidify on the surface and can be removed.

Ghee can be bought ready made. If you prefer, make it by melting unsalted butter and simmering it for 45–50 minutes until the solids brown. Strain through fine muslin or cheesecloth and refrigerate. The simmering time depends on the amount of water in the butter.

In Western dishes there are normally two or three main items in a sauce. Classic sauces are either butter and flour-based, or stock and cream may be used as a base, with the addition of wine. Apart from in the classic *bouquet garni*, or *fines herbes* mixture, herbs are often used in isolation.

Curry contrasts with this in many ways. **The base of the sauce, if non-vegetarian, is always stock.** Indians always use meat, chicken or fish on the bone (we love to chew on the meaty bones while eating) to give the curry a robust flavour. The cuts include a few gelatinous pieces as well, to give body. For extra flavour, the shank bone containing the marrow is used.

Then there is always a second base or **thickening agent** to give the curry the required consistency: this may be onions, coconut milk, ground seeds or nuts – all contribute to the flavour, besides giving body to the curry. Flour is not used as a thickening agent as it lacks flavour.

The same ingredients may play dual roles or different roles in different curries depending on how they are used and combined to achieve texture or consistency, taste, colour and flavour. For example, onions, if puréed or lightly fried, may act as a thickening agent in one curry, while in another, if browned by frying, may give a deep brown colour as well. Similarly, yoghurt may give body to one curry, but work as a souring agent in another, especially if the recipe requires the yoghurt to be a day old. So a curry recipe will be better understood if we work out the role that each ingredient plays in the recipe. The effect of each of the spices is a little complex. Spices are like musical notes. All melodies (or curries) are composed of the same musical notes (or spices).

1 **The choice of spices:** this makes the sum total of the taste and flavours.

2 **The sequence in which the spices are put into the pot** is important, as is the length of time each spice is fried and allowed to release its flavour.

3 **The ways the spices are used:** they may be fried or simply added to the boiling mixture. This is like the tone of the note – high or low. Frying releases the flavour of the spice more strongly than plain cooking.

The sequence of use of spices is important because each spice has its own pattern of releasing flavour with heat. With some this takes just a few seconds, others do better with being fried for a minute or more. If all the spices are added simultaneously, either some will burn or some will remain uncooked (or *kacha*), meaning that the flavour remains unreleased. Spices release their flavour in the most potent form in hot oil. Once moisture has been added to the mixture to which the spices are added, the release of their flavour diminishes. This includes the adding of ingredients like raw onions or tomatoes, as well as water or other liquid. For this reason onions are put in first, fried and their moisture reduced, before spices are added. So it is important to follow the recipes exactly, with the spices in the sequence mentioned, to get the flavours as they are meant to be.

For those who know a little about Indian cooking or enjoy Indian food, the importance of the word *bhuna* will be appreciated. It means frying either spices alone in oil, or meat or vegetables along with the spices, stirring continuously so that the spices are in constant contact with the hot oil and base of the pan, but do not stick. This process of **stir-frying**, which releases the flavour of the spices so effectively in the oil, is the heartbeat of a curry recipe. In some recipes spices may be put in at the next stage following the *bhuna* process, after water or ingredients containing moisture have been added. This will be done if the spices are meant to play a secondary note in the curry tune. This process also explains why Indian food in restaurants contains a lot of oil. If less oil is used in the *bhuna* process one has to stir constantly to avoid sticking, and this is labour-intensive. If enough oil is added to cover all the spices, three to four pots can be cooked at the same time, as the spices do not stick so easily. The second reason why restaurant chefs put a lot of oil into curry is that it helps the food to keep better without refrigeration if it is cooked in the morning to be served in the evening or the next day.

Many food writers and international chefs have mentioned to me that they find it mystifying how in Indian cuisine the same types of spices are common to almost every dish, unlike European food which has a different seasoning in each dish. Indian cuisine has a complexity of taste in its curry dishes, and a range of spices is used to create different tastes. It is the **relative proportion of spices,** the way they are used, as well as the **balance of spices with other flavourful ingredients,** that gives the final taste and flavour. For example, if a recipe contains a lot of red chilli, but is combined with coconut milk, the red-hot flavour is balanced with sweetness, and when the proportion of coconut is higher than that of chilli, the result is a delightful symphony of flavours.

Curries usually have one ingredient which imparts its particular characteristic **colour** and another which gives a sour tang, an important element in the complexity of flavour when combined with other ingredients. But more of that later in this chapter. Another important point to note at this stage is the **strength of the heat.** Curry was traditionally cooked over firewood or coal. Even today, the very best Indian food made by traditional cooks for important occasions will be cooked in this way in large brass or copper pots. Initially, the fire is medium-hot at the *bhuna* stage, but once this is done, the curry should be simmered on a very low fire, with the lid on so that the aromas do not escape. Traditionally at the final stage a couple of live coals are put on top of the lid so that a gentle, steady heat comes from the top as well as the bottom of the pot.

THICKENING AGENTS

Many ingredients can be used in this way, the most common being onions.

Onions

Onions are used finely or coarsely chopped, sliced or puréed. The proportion of onions to the main ingredient of the curry is important, because this will determine whether there is a sweet element in the taste as well as the thickness of the gravy. The finer the onions are cut, the less time they have to be fried or otherwise cooked in order to blend perfectly into the gravy. Onions are also puréed before frying, or sometimes cooked in their own moisture without oil to give a thicker gravy with lots of bulk. This technique is followed more in restaurants than at home, and is called 'boiled onion paste' by chefs. The longer onions are fried, the browner they will get and the deeper the colour of the curry will be. They may be deep-fried until deep brown and crispy, and then ground or blended, and added to the gravy. This gives a good flavour and consistency: see the *Lucknow Lamb Shank Korma*.

When the onions are fried only until light pink in colour, they will impart a sweetish taste to the curry. Certain varieties of onion, like Spanish onions, are too sweet to be appropriate for curry-making. The most suitable from the taste point of view are the French and the small pink English.

At the time of frying the onions, ginger and garlic are often added too. Garlic browns quicker than onions, and so it is usually added later. The exact timing is specified in each recipe.

Yoghurt

Yoghurt (always known as curd in India) gives body and a creamy texture to a curry, but Indians mostly use yoghurt as a 'souring' agent (see page 30).

Cream (*malai*) and 'hung' yoghurt

In certain dishes, particularly in the Ganges plain; cream or *malai*, as it is called in Northern India, is used. It was incorporated into later Moghlai cooking under the influence of the local cuisine of the dairy-dominated region around Faizabad and Lucknow. Similarly yoghurt is used in a concentrated form, after being left to hang in a muslin cloth, so that the whey drains away. Like this, the yoghurt does not develop a grainy texture during cooking.

Coconut milk

Coconut flesh is ground to a paste with spices, or the flesh is grated and then soaked in water for 30 minutes or blended to extract coconut milk. The first extract is thicker. The grated coconut may then be soaked in warm water to obtain a second extraction which is thinner. The second extraction can be boiled in the curry for longer than the first without releasing too much oil. When following the recipes, please do pay special attention to the details of how to use coconut milk.

Using tinned cream of coconut, shredded coconut or coconut milk powder (Nestlé's), or a bar of cream of coconut are other options. Frozen desiccated coconut often has a sweet flavour, depending on its origin, because in the West desiccated coconut is principally used in desserts. The flavour of fresh coconut is undoubtedly best, however. When buying a whole coconut, shake it to ensure that it has a little coconut water inside. This is a sign that the coconut is still fresh.

Using coconut

Coconut-based curries are *de rigueur* in the southern half of the Indian peninsula. Coconut is used in two basic ways. Either the coconut is ground (and sometimes grated and roasted before grinding) along with other spices, and the spice paste is then sautéed in oil. Or coconut milk is

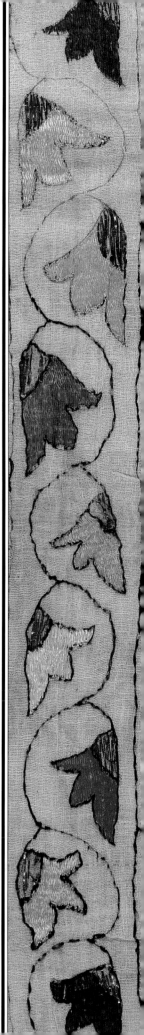

extracted by adding chopped or grated coconut to water, liquidizing it in a blender and then straining it. In this case the spices would be sautéed first, and the coconut milk added thereafter.

The taste of fresh coconut is not easy to replicate with processed products. It is unfortunate that supermarkets have not yet got round to selling freshly grated coconut (though frozen desiccated coconut is available – sometimes its taste is on the sweeter side) or freshly ground coconut, which would be so useful not only in Indian but also in Thai and Indonesian cooking. It is easy to extract coconut milk from freshly ground coconut too, by putting it into a blender with water, or just by soaking it.

I have tried dried desiccated coconut powder instead of both ground coconut and coconut milk, but it is not very effective. An exception is Nestlé's coconut powder, which is an acceptable substitute for coconut milk. There is a variation in taste between various other brands, some of which are better than others.

When using a fresh coconut, break it with a hammer or crack it open on a hard floor by hitting it. Keep a bowl handy to catch the coconut water inside. There is a superstition in Southern India that a coconut should not be broken after sundown, around 7 p.m. But at all auspicious events, a coconut is broken on the ground – the equivalent of cutting a ribbon to open an event in the Western world. After the coconut is broken, the flesh needs to be carefully separated from the shell with a strong round-ended knife. Then the dark brown skin has to be peeled off as it will not grind properly. Grating is preferable, but grinding will take a shorter time. An effective grinder should be

Chaar magaz

Almonds

White sesame seeds

Peanuts

Gram flour

Brown mustard seeds

White poppy seeds

Yoghurt

Pistachios

Half coconut

Pink onion

Cashew nuts

Lentils

Roasted grams

able to grind the coconut, even if you have to cut it into small pieces first, provided a little water (or, if the recipe demands, vinegar) is added.

A coconut-based curry cannot be stored for more than 8 hours outside a refrigerator without it going rancid. In a refrigerator it keeps for up to 2 days. There is no problem in freezing such a curry.

Nuts and Seeds

Ground almonds, cashew nuts and peanuts are sometimes used in curries, not only for their thickening quality but also for their flavour. Almonds were probably introduced into curries in India by the Moghuls and are widely used in the genuine Moghlai dishes, both of Delhi and the Ganges plain. In recent times almonds have become expensive in India, and since India is now a large-scale processor of raw cashew nuts imported from south-east Africa (Tanzania and Mozambique), cashews have begun to replace almonds fully or partially even in Moghlai dishes.

In this book, there is a *korma* made with pistachio nuts, which almost certainly has a Moghul origin.

Peanuts, which are grown widely in Gujarat, are used extensively in the cuisines of the people of the region and around Bombay, as a flavour enhancer and thickening agent in curries.

White Poppy Seeds are another favourite ingredient, primarily as a thickening agent in some Moghlai and Hyderabad dishes, and in the cuisines of the Muslim communities of Bombay and Southern India.

Mustard seeds are used as a thickener to a lesser extent. Only in a few recipes are ground mustard seeds and *methi* (fenugreek) seeds used for this purpose. In Bengal ground mustard seeds are used widely, primarily for flavour, but they do also provide the curry with body since they are used in large quantities. In the Bengali fish curry recipe in this book mustard seeds combine with poppy seeds as the thickening agent.

Pumpkin and melon seeds: another ingredient used in the court recipes of Delhi and the Ganges plain is called *chaar magaz. Chaar*, which means four, is a mixture of four kinds of seed – melon, pumpkin, squash and watermelon. These are ground with a little water into a paste, and are again used both for the body and melange of flavours they give the curry.

Sesame seeds: Til are native to India. Ground white sesame seeds feature in Western and Southern Indian cuisine and the Muslim cooking of Bombay, Hyderabad and South India, giving a unique flavour to the food. The seeds are used in small quantities and therefore not as a thickening agent on their own, but with other ingredients. Sesame seeds are widely used for making sweet dishes. These are eaten more in the winter as they are believed to have heating qualities. In Maharashtra *ladoos* or sweet round balls of sesame and *jaggery* are distributed among friends and relatives on *Makar Sankrant*, the day the sun enters Capricorn – the beginning of the winter solstice.

Lentils

Lentils (*dal*) are either ground into flour or cooked separately and then puréed for use as a thickening agent. Dishes like the Parsee *dhansak*, the North Indian *dal gosht*, Hyderabadi *dalcha*, the Bori Muslim *khichda* and the Muslim *haleem*, are all examples of meat and *dal* dishes.

Recipes for *dhansak* and *dalcha* are given in this book. The Sindhi Curry on page 152 is a vegetarian *dal* curry.

GIVING COLOUR TO A CURRY

The ingredients that give colour to a curry are:

1 Turmeric: **bright yellow.**
2 Saffron: **pale apricot.**
3 Red chillies: **reddish-brown.** The variety known as Kashmiri chilli: **vermilion.**
4 Fresh coriander leaves, if used in quantity: **green**. Darkens easily with longer cooking.
5 Red tomatoes: **pinkish** if combined with yoghurt, and **reddish** if used on their own.
6 Onions: **deep brown** if used in quantity and fried until **dark brown** without adding much water.
7 Coriander powder: **deep brown** if fried for 5–6 minutes.
8 *Garam masala* powder: **deep brown** if fried for 1 minute.

If all these are used, then the ultimate colour will depend on their proportions relative to the other ingredients used.

A field of onions in Kashmir; frying onions properly is one very important factor in curry-making

Colouring agents

Tomato

Garam masala *powder*

Deep fried onions

Cock'scomb flower

Tandoori colour

Kashmiri chilli

Saffron

Cock'scomb water

Kashmiri colour

Cock'scomb petals

Coriander powder

Turmeric

Coriander leaves

SOURING AGENTS

Since curry has a complex taste, and one of the constituent flavours is often a sour one, many curries contain a souring agent which, when used in conjunction with the hotness of chillies, and sweetness of onions, yoghurt or coconut, gives a nice tang. Souring agents are more common among the curries of the Hindus. They are absent from Moghlai dishes, with the exception of those of the Muslims of Hyderabad which incorporate the sour taste – Hyderabadi food is a wonderful mixture of Moghlai and Deccani cuisine.

Tomato

Tomatoes were brought to India by the Portuguese in the sixteenth century but began to be widely cultivated for general use only in the twentieth century. Now they are grown throughout the country all the year round. Tomatoes have become a favourite ingredient in Indian cooking for colour, flavour and the touch of sourness they give to food.

Even when ripe the Indian tomato is slightly sour in taste, compared to European or American varieties. Its acidity level is also much higher. When using tomatoes for curry-making, avoid sweeter Italian tomatoes.

Yoghurt

Yoghurt is always made at home in India, usually on a daily basis. Commercially made yoghurt is a rarity. A little live culture is mixed into milk which has been warmed, then cooled, and left overnight. The tropical climate enables the yoghurt to set easily.

Often, the Indian housewife will make a curry based on yoghurt which inadvertently went sour. To sour yoghurt specially for a particular dish, the procedure is as follows:

(a) use an already sour live culture to make the yoghurt;
(b) use slightly more of the culture, say 2 tablespoons per pint (575ml), instead of 1 tablespoon;
(c) mix the culture into the milk while the milk is still slightly warm;
(d) leave the yoghurt to set in a relatively warm place. A thermos jar which has been slightly warmed by rinsing with warm water is suitable for making yoghurt;
(e) use skimmed milk instead of full-fat milk.

When the yoghurt begins to sour, drops of water will appear on the surface and increase as the yoghurt becomes more sour. When it has reached the desired degree of sourness it is put into the refrigerator to maintain this level.

Vinegar

Vinegar in cooking is found primarily in the regions of India influenced by the Portuguese – Goa, Mangalore, Kerala – as well as in Anglo-Indian and Parsee cooking. The Indians of the West coast use a vinegar made of coconut – the closest equivalent in the West would be cider vinegar. The Parsees use molasses vinegar made from sugar cane.

Tamarind

The most popular souring agent in Southern India is the tamarind fruit, which grows on a large graceful tree. The pods are collected, de-seeded and dried. Before cooking the acid flesh is soaked in water, and the juice is squeezed out. It is this tamarind water that is used in the curry. In some Goan and Mangalorian recipes, the tamarind flesh is ground together with spices. Tamarind can be bought in any Indian grocer's and some supermarkets.

Lime

India is the original home of both the lime and the lemon, but nowadays it is the lime that is most commonly available and used, although limes are often called lemons. Thus, a so-called fresh lemon squash would actually be based on lime juice. In Hindi the lime is called the *nimbu* and is used in some curry dishes. The juice of the *nimbu* is added only at the end of the cooking process, as it would inhibit the meat from becoming tender while cooking.

Cocum

The cocum, which grows on trees along the Western coast of India, has a deep purple flesh surrounding a large seed. It imparts a pale-purplish colour to food as well as a sour taste. It is used by Sindhis in their gram flour curry, and by the Hindu Goans in their fish curries. It is also made into sherbets on the West coast of India: these refreshing drinks are made from fruits, essences and herbs, for example raw mango, fresh lime, lychees, almonds and rose. Cocum has a remarkable anti-allergic action, and a cocum infusion water drunk for three days first thing in the morning is said to cure urticaria or hives.

Raw mango

Mangoes (*kairi*) grow all over India in the summer. For two to three months before that, from about mid-March, the markets are full of bright green unripe mangoes of myriad varieties. These are used to make pickles and chutneys and finely chopped as a seasoning. During the spring 'cheeks' of raw mango are put into curries and *dals* as souring agents. Raw mango cheeks are also sun-dried and powdered and in this state are called *amchoor (aamb* meaning mango and *choor* powder). *Amchoor* is only used as a garnish, for sprinkling on fried vegetable savouries (*chaat*) or *dal*. It is not used during cooking.

Souring agents

Vinegar

Cocum

Pomegranate seeds

Sun-dried raw mango

Tomato

Lime

Yoghurt

Kaachri

Mango

Tamarind

Fish tamarind

Mango powder

THE USE OF SPICES

Curry powder in the form that it is known now in the West, was invented in Madras, to be exported to England for use by the English who had become addicted, as we have already seen, to curries. In India, spices are used in a highly individual way, and daughters learn how to use them by observing their mothers or grandmothers. Each region of India and each sub-cuisine has its own traditional palette of spices. Professional cooks in India have a great understanding of the role, possible uses and limitations of each spice. For example, pepper is used to much better effect in Kerala and the extreme south of India where it grows, while essence of the keora flower is a prized characteristic of Lucknowi cooking.

Incidentally, contrary to a widely held belief, various forms of curry powder do feature in the traditions of Indian cooking. Throughout the Western part of Maharashtra, *masala* powder (see page 37) is ground and kept for later use, though the composition of the powder varies. The *kaala masala* or black *masala* powder used in many dishes consists of pepper, clove, cinnamon and other black spices.

The East Indian Christian communities of Bombay and Bassein make a curry powder comprising about thirty spices, some very little known. Unlike commercial curry powder, it resolves the problem of some spices getting cooked while others remain under-cooked, because each spice is roasted separately for different requisite lengths of time before grinding. They make it just before the hot season and store it, tightly packed into long green bottles, for a whole year. For this reason the mixture is called 'bottled *masala*', although it is in fact a curry powder. Similarly, in March and April the Chettiars of Tamil Nadu sun-dry several spices, and onions as well, and make little marble-sized balls of curry powder rolled with oil which they also store for the entire year. These are called *kaarivadagam*: the addition of oil helps them to keep longer.

By and large, however, spices are used individually in Indian cooking. In previous centuries spices were prized for their preservative and medicinal qualities. But today dried spices are used principally for their taste and aroma in cooking and their digestive properties.

Grinding spices
This is a very important part of the curry-making process. If the spices are not ground properly the curry will have neither the correct texture nor taste. In the old days, every large household's cook had an assistant in the kitchen known as a *masaalchi*, who ground all the spice mixtures. In Indian restaurants and hotel kitchens, professional cooks guard their recipes for spice mixtures closely, putting their own proportions of the spices into grinders for apprentices to oversee.

Every home in India, however lowly, has a grinding stone. This is a piece of black granite and comes with a thick version of a rolling pin. In some parts of Southern India, the grinding stone is like a round basin with the centre scooped out and then the end of the rolling pin is used to crush the spices. A lot of pressure is required to get the spices ground to a smooth, fine consistency. Most Indians will tell you there is a vast difference in the taste between spices ground on a stone and those made in an electric mixer. A small version of the stone grinder with an electric motor is available and is principally used in Southern India to grind rice and lentils for making *idlis* and *dosas* (items in a Southern Indian breakfast) and not so much to grinding spices for curries.

In the last decade or so, a good range of electrical kitchen gadgets such as liquidizers especially suited to the preparation of Indian food has become available in India. The blades of these machines are close to the base, which enables the spices to be ground more finely than in Western grinders. Liquidizers come with two sizes of bowl, one with a very small capacity for spices and a larger one for coconut and large quantities of ingredients. The appliances do not heat up quickly as the motors are heavy-duty and therefore the spices can be ground for 10 to 15 minutes without a problem.

When selecting an appliance for grinding, a coffee grinder is useful for day-to-day grinding of spices and should be kept specifically for that purpose. For what Indians call 'wet grinding', that is, items like coconut where a little liquid is added, you need to buy a medium-sized machine with blades close to the base of the machine. This also applies to red chillies or they will not be ground to a smooth paste. Soften the chilli skins by soaking in water for 30 minutes and they will grind much better. Small herb mills are fine for grinding ginger, garlic, green chilli and coriander leaves.

SPICES USED MAINLY FOR TASTE

Coriander seeds and coriander powder (*dhania*)

The principal spice in this category is coriander powder. This is made by grinding coriander seeds. To enhance the flavour the seeds should be roasted on a hot *tawa* or griddle or frying pan without oil for 3 minutes or so, and ground just before use. This can be done in a dry grinder or coffee grinder kept specially for this purpose. Housewives and professional cooks who are particular about the taste of their curries, roast and grind coriander powder every day. Frying the coriander powder in oil gives the characteristic 'curry' flavour. It takes a minimum of 5 minutes cooking in hot oil over a low heat for the full flavour to be released from the spice into the mixture. Adding a tablespoon or two of water will not inhibit the release of flavour. Frying over a high heat means the powder will burn and become sticky more quickly. It tends to catch on the bottom of the pan unless there is a substantial amount of oil or fat, and therefore needs to be stirred continuously. If meat is being fried along with the powder, then one can stir-fry or *bhuno* the meat with powder for as long as 10 minutes without burning because there is moisture in the meat. This is the characteristic taste of a *bhuna* dish (see page 63).

Coriander seeds have diuretic properties. Coriander is grown all over India but Rajasthan and Central India produce the most. The Rajasthan variety, which is lighter brown in colour, is also the most flavourful with a good aroma. It is mostly this variety that is used in India to make commercial coriander powder. The coriander from around Indore in Central India has a greenish tinge and is mostly used in seed form.

The coriander sold in the UK is also imported from North Africa and Eastern Europe.

Turmeric (*haldi*)

This is a root and is mostly used as a powder made from the dried root. Fresh turmeric root, available from December to March in India, gives an even better colour and flavour than dried. Turmeric is difficult to powder at home, and there is always a danger of buying an adulterated form in markets, so shrewd housewives buy their annual requirements before the summer and get it pounded in their presence. Turmeric has antiseptic qualities and is therefore used to marinate fish before cooking, particularly by the Hindus. In the making of curries, turmeric is used more by the Hindus than the Muslims, who avoid using it in many recipes. It sticks very easily to the bottom of the pan during frying, but needs only a few seconds of frying to release its flavour, does not burn quickly and can therefore be added at any point in the frying sequence, even if only spices are being fried, without meat, fish or vegetable. The largest turmeric production is around the town of Erode in Tamil Nadu, in Andhra and Maharashtra. That which gives the brightest hue is from the area around Allepey in Kerala. The biggest turmeric market in the world is in Sangli, where the turmeric is stored in large pits in the ground.

Dried red chilli and chilli powder

These are explained in detail in a separate section. When adding chilli powder in a curry recipe, do so during the second half of the frying sequence if only spices are fried, as within a few seconds or so chilli emits pungent vapours which make you cough. Fried with meat or chicken it can comfortably be cooked along with other spices like coriander and turmeric for 10 minutes. If you are frying chilli on its own and get a singeing aroma, add a little water.

Cumin seeds (*jeera*)

Cumin seeds are used whole or ground as powder. Again, it should be roasted very briefly for only a minute on a hot *tawa* or griddle and then ground into a powder to release its flavour more fully. Whole or powdered *jeera* burns quicker than most spices and turns black quickly and becomes bitter, and should therefore be fried for less than half a minute or until you see it is turning a blackish colour, at which point add the next ingredient, be it tomato, yoghurt, or any other ingredient containing moisture. Then the burning process will stop. Cumin seeds are used in the cooking of dry vegetable dishes like *jeera aloo* (with potatoes). Fried in a little oil and made into a *wagar* or seasoning, the seeds are sprinkled on top of boiled rice or *dal*.

Cumin is considered to be a digestive. The drink known as *jeera paani* or cumin water, is basically an infusion of cumin, lime juice and fresh coriander leaves. It also has 'cooling' properties.

Cinnamon and cloves (*tuj/dalchini* and *lavang*)

These spices contribute to both taste and aroma but have a specially strong impact on taste. They are used whole in some meat recipes, and along with green cardamom when boiling rice to make a simple *pulao*, or ground together with black cardamom and made into a *garam masala* powder (see page 37). Commercial *garam masala* powder exists but is by no means always ideal, because many manufacturers tend to skimp on using the expensive ingredients and add inessential cheaper ones to increase the volume. Many housewives prefer the flavour of homemade *garam masala*.

Cinnamon is a thinner, tan-coloured bark, while cassia is a rougher, dark brown bark. Often what is sold in the name of cinnamon is actually cassia bark, so be sure to buy a good brand of cinnamon. Cassia has a sweeter taste than cinnamon.

The whole spices can be fried for a few minutes without burning. Cinnamon can be fried for 5 minutes, and cloves for under 2 minutes if there are no other ingredients with moisture. If roasting them dry in a powdered form with other spices, allow under 2 minutes over a low heat.

Green chillies

Garlic

Ginger

Coriander seeds

Coriander powder

Red chillies

Cinnamon leaves

Chilli powder

Turmeric powder

Cumin seeds

Cumin powder

Principal Spices for Making a Curry

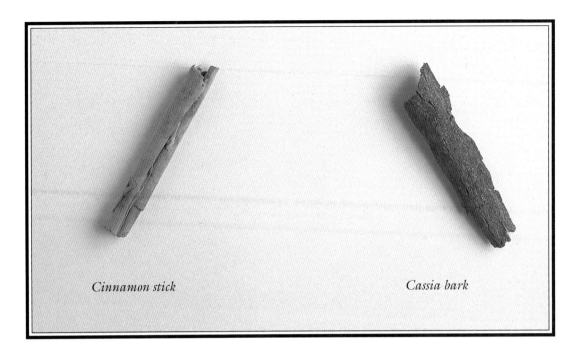

Cinnamon stick   *Cassia bark*

It is not essential that cinnamon and cloves be fried, though this releases the flavour better into the oil. They can, however, be successfully added directly to a curry or rice mixture. Clove is a strong spice, and just 2 or 3 in a dish give a perceptible flavour. Cloves burn faster than cinnamon, and should always be put in after cinnamon.

Pepper (*kali mirchi*)

Pepper grows mainly in Kerala. It was a highly prized item in world trade as far back as the second century AD, when pepper from Malabar was exported to Rome in exchange for gold. Christopher Colombus set off on his journey of discovery in search of the source of pepper and cloves. In those days pepper was especially prized for its preservative qualities.

Peppercorns boiled in water along with Indian basil leaves (*tulsi*) is drunk in India as an infusion to cure a cold in the chest or asthma. Pepper is used lavishly in Kerala cooking. When frying the peppercorn is always used whole and should be fried for not more than 1 minute, if no other ingredient with moisture is present.

In India, spices cooked whole do not dissolve during the cooking of a curry, and Indians are quite used to them appearing on their plate or in their mouths and will discretely put them aside. They can be tied in a muslin bag during cooking and removed from the pan after frying.

Mustard seeds (*rai* or *sarson*)

Mustard seeds are used whole in Southern Indian curries and vegetable dishes, almost always as the first ingredient to be fried for a few seconds in the cooking oil. Mustard seeds are the favourite spice of Bengal, where mustard grows in abundance; the seeds are ground into a paste and used to flavour Bengali fish dishes. Mustard oil is also widely used in Bengal and Kashmir. In the Punjab, the leaves of the mustard plant are a favourite winter vegetable.

If frying mustard seeds whole, do so for 10–15 seconds when they will begin to splutter and crackle. Then add the next spice or ingredient according to the recipe. In Indian cooking the use of mustard powder or prepared mustard is insignificant, though the latter if added to some curry preparations could enhance the taste. So feel free to innovate.

The most commonly used mustard seeds are black (*rai*), though in the North and East of the country, reddish-brown ones (*sarson*) are used.

Fenugreek seeds (*methi*)

These are usually used whole, and only in a few recipes. In Southern Indian cuisine, *methi* seeds are the second ingredient after mustard seeds to be put in hot oil and fried for a few seconds before the other ingredients are added. They are also used roasted and powdered along with red chilli and other spices in a condiment mix known as *muligapuri*, to be eaten with *idli* and *dosas*.

Poppy seeds (*khus khus*)

These are almost always used in a curry ground to a paste with a little water. They do not grind easily and should be lightly toasted on a griddle for 3–4 minutes, then ground in a coffee grinder with a little water added if necessary. They have a very mild flavour. Used as a coating for potatoes and fried savoury items they impart a nutty taste, as they do to curry, in which they are used as a thickening agent.

Fennel (*saunf*)

This sometimes forms part of *garam masala* powder. Fennel powder features in Kashmiri cuisine, both Hindu and Muslim, and is also used by the Mapla Muslims of Kerala. It is not essential to fry fennel powder as it is very aromatic. In Kashmiri curries, fennel powder is always used without the frying process. In Chettinad cuisine whole fennel seeds are used as one of the main spices.

Many Indian cookery books mention aniseed as a spice, but actually it is fennel that is being referred to – there is no aniseed in Indian cuisine.

SPICES USED MAINLY FOR AROMA

It is very difficult to distinguish spices used principally for taste and those for aroma, as all spices will affect both. However, some have a marginally greater effect on taste and others on aroma, and for those who are not very familiar with spices, this distinction can help to make it easier to appreciate the role of each spice a little better. Some, like the *garam masala* spices, affect taste if fried in the initial mixture, but contribute to the aroma in a stronger way if sprinkled on in powder form towards the end of the cooking process. The spices which contribute more to aroma are detailed in this section.

Garam masala

As mentioned above, *garam masala* contributes to both flavour and aroma, but I feel the latter is predominant. *Garam* means 'heating' in this context (though in Hindi the literal translation is 'hot'). *Masala*, of course, refers to the spices. So *garam masala* is a mixture of those spices which create heat in the body – cinnamon, cloves, black pepper and black cardamom. Interestingly, the first two were exported to India at the time of the spice trade! Nowadays housewives making *garam masala* mixture sometimes include the 'cooling' green cardamom, the *tej patta* or Indian bay leaf, and fennel (*saunf*). Master chefs use a wide array of spices, including dried rose petals. Every recipe for *garam masala* powder is different. To get the best flavour, grind a small quantity in a coffee grinder just before use.

Garam masala is used mostly with meat and to a lesser extent in poultry and rice dishes. It is rarely used in fish or vegetable dishes because its aroma is considered to be too strong for these.

Garam masala powder

Commercial whole garam masala mix

Cloves

Cinnamon

Black peppercorns

Ingredients for garam masala

Large black cardamom

Making your own *garam masala:*

Indian housewives always buy whole *garam masala* spices (cinnamon sticks, cloves, peppercorns and black cardamom pods, sometimes cumin and coriander seeds), then toast them on a griddle and pound them into a powder in a mortar with a pestle. Nowadays, Indian food processors have a small attachment (like a coffee grinder) for dry-grinding small quantities of spices, so pounding is no longer necessary.

There are two ways to make your own. One is to buy everything whole and proceed as above. Or you can buy everything ready-powdered, and mix the spices thoroughly in a bowl with a spoon.

A classic *garam masala* would have approximately equal quantities in weight of cinnamon, cloves and black pepper, with a little black cardamom. The rest depends on individual preference. I like to add fennel seeds and a touch of cinnamon leaf.

So, if using whole spices, take 6 grams of cinnamon (this is a lot of cinnamon, which is very light), 6 grams each of cloves and pepper and 1 black cardamom (2 grams). You can add 1 teaspoon of fennel seeds and 1 cinnamon or bay leaf.

Alternatively, take 2½ teaspoons cinnamon powder, 1 teaspoon each of clove powder and black pepper and ¾ teaspoon of fennel powder. Then grind one black cardamom and a cinnamon or bay leaf together and add this powder to the mixture.

Store *garam masala* in a tightly sealed bottle in the refrigerator, where it will keep for 6 months if you have used fresh spices to start with, though from the flavour point of view it is better to use it within 3 months.

Cinnamon leaf (*tej* or *tuj patta*)

Tej in Hindi means sharp and *patta* means leaf. So it is presumed in India that *tej patta* refers to the leaf with a sharp and strong flavour. But *tej* is actually a corruption of the word *tuj* in Gujarati (the language used in Bombay, India's largest spice city) which means cinnamon, so *tej patta* is the cinnamon-flavoured leaf from a tree which is similar to the cinnamon tree.

Cinnamon is part of the same botanical family Lauraceae as the Mediterranean bay tree (the *Laurus nobilis*) but true cinnamon is *cinnamomum zeylenicum*; cassia, which is similar in flavour to cinnamon, is *cinnamomum aromaticum*; and the *tej patta* leaf is *cinnamomum tamala*. It grows in North-East India, and in Kerala.

The *tej patta* leaf is usually fried in the initial stages of making a curry and does not burn even if fried over a low to medium heat for 10 minutes, as it browns and releases its flavour gradually. It can also be put in a boiling gravy or rice. Before serving remove it from the cooking pot.

The Indian cinnamon leaf is not presently available in the West, but the Mediterranean bay leaf can be used in its place.

Large black cardamom (*barra elaichi*)

Barra means large and this cardamom is about 6–8 times the size of the small green cardamom. Black cardamom is used only in Indian curries, and is grown in North-East India and Sikkim. It has a strong aroma, the flavour being in its seeds. It is used in small quantities and should form a part of any recipe for *garam masala* powder.

If black cardamom is used whole it should be removed from the pot before serving. If only the seeds are used, pound before using and they will dissolve into the food during cooking. Black cardamom, featured in several recipes in this book, is available from Indian grocery shops.

Green cardamom (*elaichi powder*)

Green cardamom, apart from having a unique aroma, also contributes to flavour. Avoid using white cardamom which is a bleached version of the green variety and has less flavour. Powder made from the whole green cardamom, sprinkled at the end of the cooking process on a delicate lamb or mutton dish just a few minutes before serving, gives a wonderful aroma (the dish should be kept covered). This can be done even if whole or crushed cardamoms have already been used in the cooking, because by the end, when a number of spices have been used, no single aroma will predominate.

Cardamom in crushed form is also used in sweet dishes like *shrikand* (flavoured hung yoghurt), and in cooling drinks like the almond-flavoured *thandai*. Cardamom has cooling properties even though some housewives put it in their *garam masala*.

Nutmeg (*jaiphal*)

Nutmeg originates from the Moluccas in Indonesia and in earlier times was exported to India. Today it is grown in Kerala.

Nutmeg is used sparingly in Indian cooking, in both curries and sweet dishes. Always used in its powdered form, it is normally added during the cooking process, and is not fried along with the main spices. Try putting *jaiphal* powder on puréed spinach – it transforms the dish.

Green cardamom

Mace Powder (*javitri*)

Mace is the net-like covering of nutmeg. Like cardamom, powdered mace gives a wonderful aroma when sprinkled on meat dishes towards the end of cooking, and on *pulao* dishes in which rice is cooked along with the other main ingredient, for example lamb or mixed vegetables. It is a favourite condiment among the Muslim court cooks of Lucknow, who use it during the cooking of hot *kormas* as well as sprinkling it on the top when the dish is almost ready. It is important to keep the lid on, so that the aroma is incorporated in the dish, aided by the heat within.

Asafoetida (*hing*)

This is a seasoning used primarily as an anti-flatulent, and has a strong aroma. It is a resin from the plant *ferula asafoetadia*, imported mainly from Iran. Minute quantities are used in cooking.

Star aniseed (*chakraphool* or *badian*)

This is a native of China and is not commonly used in Indian cooking. Its widest use is in Kashmir and Chettinad cooking – the Chettiar community of the South-East coast of India traded with China and South West Asia for many hundreds of years. It is also incorporated in the East Indian bottled *masala*, and in a few Goan dishes.

Saffron (*kesar*)

Saffron has a delicate fragrance, and is the most expensive spice in the world. It is the stigma of a flower of the crocus family which originated in West Asia and grows in Kashmir and Turkey, and in Mediterranean countries – the largest quantity now comes from Spain. The use of saffron is very much part of Indian cooking, especially in Moghlai dishes since it was a favourite ingredient in the Moghul courts. It is now popular in India for *biryanis, pulaos, kesari* chicken (a creamy saffron curry dish) and desserts such as *kesari kulfi*. Saffron comes in strands which need to be soaked in a little warm water or milk to infuse. It also gives off a golden-yellow dye which imparts a pale yellow hue to white rice or a milk-based dessert. It loses its flavour after a month, and is best stored tightly sealed in a refrigerator.

Powdered rose petals (*gulab*)

Powdered rose petals are used for their aroma and marinade qualities when cooking meat dishes. This tradition can be seen today in the Lucknowi court dishes, particularly in light-coloured delicate *kormas* such as the white *korma*. The Indian rose is small with a double row of petals, and has a much more intense fragrance than Western roses. The best-quality Indian roses for culinary purposes are the small ones (*gulabs*) from the Udaipur region (where they were specially cultivated to make a rose liqueur called *Gulab*), from Mysore and near Kanauj in North India. The rose petals are sun-dried and then powdered for use in cooking. *Gulab* has cooling properties, and is also astringent and anti-inflammatory. Rose essence is used in making sherbets. Rose water is used for sprinkling, after cooking, on *biryanis* and *pulaos*, and also for soaking saffron.

Screwpine flower essence (*Keora essence*)

Pandanus odoratissimus is a yellow flower from the screwpine family, with a very strong, sweet aroma. The male flowers are valued for their fragrance. It grows in Orissa and to a lesser degree in Kerala. Keora (sometimes spelt as Kewda) *attar* and Keora water are made using an extraction of this flower. Keora oil is believed to be a stimulant.

Keora *attar* is made for culinary purposes in Lucknow, and just a drop diluted in a little water before using is enough to flavour 2¼lb (1kg) of meat. A more diluted version of this is Keora water. Lucknow cooks use it in *biryanis,* kebabs and *kormas,* and are now being imitated by Muslim cooks all over India.

Aromatic spices

Caraway seeds

Fenugreek seeds

White poppy seeds

cumin seeds

Green cardamom

Wild onion seeds

Fennel seeds

Mace

Nutmeg

Star anise

Dried rose petals

Black mustard seeds

Asafoetida

Triphala

Yellow mustard seeds

HERBS AND
FRESH SPICES

The term *hara masala,* meaning literally 'green spices', refers to fresh ginger, garlic, green chillies, fresh coriander leaves, curry leaves, fenugreek leaves, mint, lime, spring onions and any other herbs, such as fresh dill. Most curries will contain *hara masala* in one form or another. In the vegetable markets there are vendors who specialize only in the sale of these herbs.

Almost all curry recipes include **ginger** and **garlic**. The traditional method is to chop them finely and fry them along with the onions. They are usually used together, often in almost equal quantities. Someone once explained to me that this is so because, while ginger tends to raise blood pressure, garlic is good for keeping it low, and so both are used to maintain an even keel. I do not know how much credence can be given to this theory, but there it is.

Professional restaurant cooks now make a purée of equal quantities of ginger and garlic either together or separately, and this can be stored in a refrigerator (covered, please remember) for several days. Housewives are increasingly beginning to do the same for the sake of convenience.

There are two varieties of garlic in India which I have not seen anywhere else. One is called *taaza lasan* (fresh garlic) and is a plant about 7 in (17.5 cm) high with a single garlic clove at the tip of its root. Very popular in Bombay in the winter, it is used by the Sindhis to flavour fish dishes, by the Parsees in scrambled egg, and in mincemeat by the Boris. It is the young shoots of the normal garlic plant grown in sandy soil. Another form of garlic is a tiny bead-like pod which the vegetable sellers say is good for the heart!

Varieties of Indian garlic

Ginger is almost always used fresh – it keeps well for a couple of months, particularly in a cold place. Powdered ginger is used mostly in Kashmir and in *chaat* preparations in North India.

Fresh coriander leaves are used both as an ingredient at the beginning of cooking and at the end as a decorative and aromatic garnish. They are also one of the main ingredients in a green curry. Coriander leaves, mint, ginger, lime juice and sugar blended together in a mixer makes a delicious fresh green chutney.

Garlic

Dill

Coriander

Kashmiri shallots

Fenugreek

Green chillies

African chilli

Curry leaves

Red chillies

Whole pod garlic

Ginger

Fresh garlic

Fresh mint

Fenugreek

Mint is used in cooking, particularly in making *dhansak* and *biryani*, but is added towards the end in order to retain the flavour. Mint should not be fried along with the *masala* as it turns black quite quickly and will give a blackish colour to the curry.

Curry leaf is a herb used only in Southern and Western coast cooking of India from Bombay down to Kerala, though it is absent in Goan cooking. It is very fragrant and can be fried in the initial stages or put in at the simmering stage. Added at the final stage of a curry, it will retain maximum flavour, but it needs to cook for at least 5 minutes. It is used in dry dishes, *dals, khadis,* in yoghurt and vegetable dishes, in meat curries and in some fish curries of Kerala and Madras. When dried, the curry leaves have very little flavour.

Curry leaf is from the same botanical family as the neem tree, the leaves of which have anti-bacterial properties, and is used as a natural pesticide.

Fenugreek *(methi)* leaves are used only in Indian cooking. There are two varieties of *methi* – the small one, about 3 in (7.5 cm) high with tiny bud-like leaves, has a more delicate flavour but has a very short season in the summer. The larger *methi* leaf is about 10 in (25 cm) high and is available throughout the year. It is very easy to grow from seed. The small *methi* is actually the young shoots of the larger *methi*, but grown in sandy soil. It has a far more intense and fragrant flavour and is available only in Bombay and Western India.

Methi leaves have a unique flavour with a slightly bitter tinge and are an acquired taste. A favourite Indian dish is *methi aloo*, or potatoes made in quite dry *karai* flavoured with *methi*. A recipe is given in this book. *Methi* leaves are used throughout India. The Punjabis put it in many dishes, including Chicken Makhani, the Parsees use it in *dhansak*, and the favourite Sindhi style of preparing fish is with fresh single-cloved garlic (they call it *thoom)* and *methi* leaves.

Methi is also sold dried, in packets known as *kasuri methi,* in most Indian grocery shops. It is quite strong in flavour, and only a pinch of it should be used in a dish. The dry *methi* is not the same botanical species as the fresh one.

Dill *(sooaa)* is used to flavour spinach and other leafy green vegetables, and *dhansak*. The Sindhis have a green spinach dish known as *sai bhaji* and also make a dill-flavoured rice, for which the recipe is also given in this book.

Using a ladle to fry spices

Chillies

It is important to understand the use of chillies in the making of curries, since they are an important ingredient and their use is limited in the West. Chillies are becoming increasingly popular in some parts of America however, largely because of the influence of Mexican cuisine, in which a variety of chillies are used.

In Indian cooking two kinds of chilli are used – the **green** variety which is used fresh and the **red**, used in dried form. The varieties of green chilli differ in their size (length) and pungency. Therefore, quantities of green chillies in a recipe are only indicative. If a curry is meant to be pungent the recipe will say so, and if the particular chillies you are using are not very hot, you should increase the number, and vice versa.

Chillies are always most pungent when raw, and mellow when fried or braised. Therefore, though the recipes may appear to contain many chillies, the finished dishes will not be as hot as they first appeared. Chillies are a valuable source of vitamin C and are good for digestion. In India they are eaten raw, as in a *cachumber* salad or a fresh green chutney, as well as cooked, and are included in almost all savoury preparations.

Red chillies are sometimes used in addition to green chillies in curries, for their hot taste and to give a reddish colour. On the Western and Southern coasts of India the skin of the red chilli is ground together with coconut to give the curry texture.

The correct use of red chillies is vital if one wants to make gourmet-style curries. The Indian housewife cooks in the culinary style of her own region and when shopping buys the locally available chilli, without perhaps being aware of its origin. It was only when I began to cook the recipes that I had gathered from different parts of India in my kitchen in Bombay that I realized that the original taste was missing and that this difference was due to the variation in chillies used elsewhere in the country. But cookery books, restaurants and home cooks in India rarely specify the use of different chillies in the different regional recipes. The only exception is the so-called **Kashmiri chilli** which is often mentioned because in recent years it has become popular as the variety that gives bright red colour and at the same time is mildly hot in taste. I say 'so-called' because when I tried to trace the origin of the Kashmiri chilli in the wholesale chilli markets in India, I found that Kashmir itself did not export the quantities of Kashmiri chillies being sold everywhere, and a similar variety was being cultivated in northern Karnataka, the region east of Goa, and in Andhra, and was widely sold all over India as Kashmiri chilli! So, if substituting for the Kashmiri chilli, look for the type that is the length of a finger and gives more bright red colour than 'bite'. The New Mexico chilli is a good substitute, though its powder or purée does not have the bright colour of the Indian Kashmiri type.

India is the largest world producer of chillies, annual production being in the order of 80,000 tonnes: only about 25,000 tonnes are exported. There is a growing export trade of spice oils and oleoresins (essential extracts) of chillies for the bulk food business, for which chillies with the best colour are used. Chillies are grown throughout the country for local use, but for cash crops the largest producers are Maharashtra, Tamil Nadu (the Madras variety), Andhra (the Guntur variety being the most pungent and therefore largely used for commercially sold red chilli powder), Karnataka (the Bedgi and Kashmiri variety) and Rajasthan. Kashmir grows its bright red and fragrant chillies largely for home consumption, as the hilly terrain makes it commercially unviable

Kashmiri chillies

*So-called
Kashmiri chillies
(dubby)*

to transport it. Goa also grows its own large-size chilli, which is ideal for the Goa curry, but even the Goans have developed a fascination for using the Kashmiri variety. The gourmets of Northern India use a bright yellow dried chilli grown around the Sonepat area in Punjab for their white or yellow curry dishes.

Recipes indicate whether green chillies are to be used whole, slit or chopped, as the manner of cutting the chilli affects the pungency of the curry. A slit chilli imparts some pungency to the curry, the whole chilli much less. Some dishes call for broken-up red chilli, others for it to be ground into a paste with a little water or vinegar, while in other recipes only red chilli powder is to be used. The stalks of chillies are always removed before use.

To achieve the bright colour effect of red chilli powder with a less hot taste, it can be mixed with paprika. Similarly, to reduce the pungency of red or green chillies, de-seed them before using. Remember to do this under running water, using gloves if your hands are sensitive, and to wash your hands thoroughly with soap immediately afterwards.

The recipes in this book mention the use of a particular chilli if it is vital to the taste. I hope that before long grocery shops and supermarkets outside India will become increasingly particular about the chillies they sell, and manufacturers will respond to the market and supply the chilli variety specified, both whole and in powdered form.

Some red chillies

Single Reshampatti

Yellow

Double Reshampatti

Byadgi

True Kashmiri

So-called Kashmiri

Goan

Tinnevelly

Guntur red

Nellore

THE CURRY PICTURE

Starting Point	Name of Curry	Colour	Thickening Agent	Dominant Spice	Supporting Spice	Souring Agent	Chilli to be used	To be eaten with
1 Want to have a mild fish curry.	Fish curry in coconut milk – fish molee	Pale yellow	Coconut milk	Ginger	Clove Cinnamon Cardamom	–	Slit green chillies	White rice Tomato rice Green rice
2 Want to have lamb to eat with sliced bread.	Seyal Gosht	Light brown	Onions and yoghurt	Coriander powder	Whole cloves Cinnamon Cardamom	Yoghurt & tomatoes	Fresh green and red chilli powder	*Pulao* rice or sliced bread or *paratha*
3 Want to have a mild chicken curry without coconut to have with rice and/or *roti*.	Kashmiri Chicken Korma	Ochre	Onion	Cardamoms Cinnamon	Ginger powder Cloves	Yoghurt	Green chillies	Any rice or *roti*
4 Want to combine meat or chicken with lentils and vegetables, eat it with rice and not have to make a side dish. Also should be able to keep it in a fridge for the next day.	Dhansak	Deep greenish brown	Lentils	Coriander Cumin powder	Fenugreek leaves Cloves Cinnamon	Lime juice Tamarind	Fresh green and red chilli powder	Brown *pulao* rice Green coconut chutney Onion and tomato *cachumber* Fried *papadums*
5 Want to make a simple curry to cater for both vegetarians and non-vegetarians without having to go through two recipes.	Goa curry – seafood or chicken and mixed veg.	Orangey red	Ground coconut	Coriander Chilli	Coriander Turmeric	Tamarind (can also use vinegar)	Bright red Kashmiri type, dried red chilli or red chilli powder and paprika powder	White rice

Chilli powders

49

HINTS & SHORT CUTS

Cut and prepare all the ingredients before you begin to cook. In Indian food particularly, there are so many ingredients that it is useful if they can be kept ready to use. If you have a large herb and spice collection, take out the ones needed for the dish in question and keep them handy.

If you are cooking for a party you can cook the curry and the *dal* a day ahead, though the *dal* should not be seasoned until shortly before serving. The vegetables can be cut and kept aside, a day in advance, but ideally should be cooked not more than a few hours beforehand. The same applies to the *raita*, for which the yoghurt should be fresh. The bread dough for the *rotis* can be made a day ahead. The *rotis* themselves can be made a couple of hours ahead, spread with a little butter and wrapped in kitchen foil, then reheated in an oven just before serving. The chutney can be made a day ahead and stored in the refrigerator, though tomato chutney can be kept for a week. The *cachumber* should be made just about an hour before the party, and the *papadams* cooked.

Curries of meat and chicken can be successfully frozen, but the texture of cooked fish suffers a little. Cooked lentils, chickpeas and vegetables freeze well.

If you are short of time and want to cook very quickly without having to peel and cut, use bottled ginger and garlic purée (the latter comes in tubes too), tinned tomato purée and tinned cream of coconut where the recipe demands it. However, there is no short-cut for browned onions except to fry them in batches and freeze them.

Many housewives in India and outside peel and purée ginger and garlic, sometimes green chilli too, and store it in jars in the refrigerator, which enables them to cook in a hurry.

Avoid using a sweet variety of onions. It is important that the moisture content is not too high – the ones in India are ripened fast and do not have a sweet taste. The recipes in this book have been adapted for onions grown in the West; those to avoid particularly are the sweet Spanish varieties.

Most of the recipes mention fresh tomatoes. If using canned tomatoes, they will give a better colour to the curry, but you may have to increase the quantity of the souring ingredient if there is one in the curry and also the salt and chilli, if necessary.

MISHAPS

1 If the onions burn while browning, remove all the burnt bits, change the pot and add a little fresh oil, otherwise the burnt taste will pervade the curry. You may have to start again.

2 If the curry has become too hot, and contains tomatoes and/or whipped yoghurt, or coconut milk, add an extra tomato or two. Also add ½–1 teaspoon of sugar. If the curry is a sour one, increase the souring agent.

3 If the curry has become too salty, add pieces of potato, or a piece of dough which you must remove before serving. The potatoes and dough will absorb the liquid and then you can top up with a cup of plain water which will dilute the saltiness.

4 If the curry is too liquid, boil uncovered (keep your extractor hood on!) for a few minutes.

5 If the curry is not spicy enough, fry whatever spices you like with some chopped green chilli in hot oil in a little saucepan or ladle (be careful as the chilli can splutter) and add to the curry.

MAKING A SIMPLE HOMESTYLE CURRY

OR THE FIRST LESSON IN MAKING A CURRY

Before attempting the curry recipes in this book you may like to start with the simplest way of making a homestyle curry, as follows. You can substitute fresh ginger and garlic, with one teaspoon of bottled ginger/garlic purée. (If cooking for 1, put the remaining half in the fridge or freezer.)

Curry for 2:

Chicken curry
1lb (450g) poussin or
2 breast fillets or
4 thighs or
6 drumsticks

Lamb curry
10 oz (300g) stewing lamb

Fish curry
2 fillets of cod, about 8oz (225g) or
2 salmon steaks

Vegetable curry
8oz (225g) mixed diced vegetables

Curry sauce
4 tablespoons oil
1 large onion, very finely chopped
2 cloves garlic, chopped
¼-in (5-mm) square piece of fresh
  ginger, chopped
¾ teaspoon coriander powder
a pinch of turmeric powder
¼ teaspoon cumin powder
¼ teaspoon *garam masala* powder
1 teaspoon paprika powder
2 tomatoes, chopped
salt
chopped coriander leaves to garnish

1 Heat the oil in a heavy pan. Add the onion and sauté over a medium heat for about 20–25 minutes or until deep brown. Add the garlic and ginger and fry for 1 minute. Add the coriander powder and stir for a further full minute. Then add the turmeric, cumin, *garam masala* and paprika and sauté for 30 seconds. Add 1 cup water and cook for 10 minutes. Put in the tomatoes, stir well and cook for a further 5 minutes.

2 Now the curry sauce is ready. Add salt to taste. Put in the chicken, lamb, fish or vegetables. Add 1½ cups water for the chicken, 2½ cups for the lamb, 1 cup for the fish, 2 cups for the vegetables. Cook until done. Sprinkle with chopped coriander leaves just before serving.

Eat with rice, pitta bread or on sliced bread.

THE CURRIES

ROGAN JOSH

(KASHMIR)

Rogan means meat fat and *josh* literally means heat, though figuratively it means intensity. Traditionally fatty meat on the bone was used for making *Rogan Josh* and it was slow-cooked in its own fat, with extra added for an intense flavour. In these days of cholesterol-consciousness, however, we avoid animal fat and use a minimum amount of oil. The dish gets its heat and intensity from the lavish use of body heat-inducing spices such as large black cardamoms and cloves.

The hallmark of the dish as cooked in Kashmir is the liberal use of the true Kashmiri red chilli, which has a mild flavour but gives a bright red colour. The Muslims there use *praan*, a Kashmiri shallot, that has a garlicky flavour, and *maval*, the petals of the cock'scomb flower. The latter gives the curry an even brighter red colour and is supposed to have cooling properties. The Hindus of Kashmir do not use *praan* or any onion or garlic but give body or flavour to the curry by the addition of yoghurt. The spice distinguishing Kashmiri *Rogan Josh* from those made in other parts of India is fennel powder.

I have combined the recipes of both the Hindu and Muslim communities and replaced exotic ingredients with those which are easily available. The curry is mildly spicy and has a ravishing flavour. It is traditionally eaten with boiled rice but can also be eaten with *rotis* or a saffron *pulao*.

Serves 4	4 cloves
	2 large black cardamoms
1½lb (700g) stewing lamb or chops	4 green cardamoms
9oz (250g) lamb bones for adding flavour	2 cinnamon or bay leaves
4 cloves garlic, chopped	1 blade of mace
2½ teaspoons chilli powder (preferably Kashmiri)	1 teaspoon coriander powder
or 2 teaspoons chilli powder and 1 teaspoon paprika	1 teaspoon fennel powder
½ cup full-fat yoghurt	1 teaspoon ginger powder
9oz (250g) shallots, chopped	¼ teaspoon turmeric powder
¼ cup ghee or oil	salt to taste – about 1¼ teaspoons

1 Boil the lamb and bones with the garlic and ½ teaspoon salt in 6 cups water in a cooking pot for 20 minutes. Remove from the heat. Remove the meat and set aside. Skim off the scum and strain and reserve the cooking liquor.

2 Make a paste of chilli powder and/or paprika by mixing with a little water. Whisk the yoghurt and set aside.

3 Fry the shallots in the *ghee* or oil in a pot until lightly browned (this will take about 12 minutes). Add cloves, cardamoms, cinnamon or bay leaves and the mace and fry for 1 minute. Then add the coriander, fennel, ginger and turmeric powders, and the chilli paste and 2 tablespoons water and stir continuously. After 2 minutes add the meat. Sauté for about 5 minutes. Lower the heat and add the yoghurt, stir well and sauté for a few minutes.

4 Add salt to taste, together with 4 cups water. Cook until the meat is tender. Before serving, remove the cinnamon or bay leaves, the large cardamoms and mace if intact.

LAMB WITH TURNIPS

SHALGAM GOSHT (KASHMIR)

In the winter in Kashmir, turnips (*shalgam*) with a lovely mauvish tinge are one of the few vegetables available. They are stored in pits dug in the snow. This variety of turnip is the size of a medium onion, and grows throughout North India.

Shalgam Gosht is popular in Lucknow too.

The Kashmiri red chilli gives the dish a wonderful red colour, which can also be achieved by using a blend of red chilli powder and good paprika, as a substitute. The large black cardamom, which is considered to be heat-producing in the body – good in the winter! – gives it a nice aroma, as does the powdered fennel. The salt rubbed on the turnips before frying removes their bitterish taste.

Serves 4

11oz (300g) small turnips	5 tablespoons oil
salt	1 teaspoon red chilli powder
14oz (400g) small onions	1½ teaspoons paprika powder
2 garlic cloves	1 teaspoon turmeric powder
1½-in (4-cm) piece fresh ginger	¾ teaspoon fennel powder
9oz (250g) medium tomatoes	1½ teaspoons coriander powder
about 9oz (250g) lamb bones for stock	2 black cardamoms
1 bay leaf	4 green cardamoms
	1½-in (4-cm) cinnamon stick
	1½lb (700g) stewing lamb, cut into pieces

1   Peel the turnips and cut into quarters. Prick each piece several times with a toothpick. Sprinkle with a little salt and run in well. Leave at room temperature to degorge for at least 1 hour, then rinse off the salt and set the turnips aside.

2   Chop the onions, 1 clove of garlic and the ginger. Cut the tomatoes in half and grate, discarding the skin. Alternatively purée the peeled tomatoes in a blender.

3   Make a stock by boiling the lamb bones for 45 minutes in 2 cups of water along with the remaining clove of garlic and the bay leaf, and strain.

4   In a frying pan heat 3 tablespoons of the oil and fry the turnips for about 20 minutes until they are pale gold in colour and beginning to get a crispy skin. Keep turning them around so they become evenly pale gold in colour. Remove the turnips and drain on kitchen paper.

5   Put the oil from the pan into a cooking pot. Add 1 tablespoon of the remaining oil. Add the chopped onions and sauté for about 20–25 minutes over a low to moderate heat until golden-brown. Make sure the heat is not too high or they will fry unevenly. Then add the chopped ginger and garlic and continue to sauté for a further 5 minutes.

6   Add the chilli, paprika, turmeric, fennel and coriander powders, the cardamoms, cinnamon, 2 tablespoons water, the remaining 1 tablespoon of oil and the lamb, and mix well. Stir-fry the meat for 2 minutes so that it is evenly coated with spices. Cover the pot and simmer for about 10 minutes until the meat releases moisture which mingles with the spices and is re-absorbed.

7   Remove lid when the meat is almost dry. Then, with a cooking spoon, stir and turn the meat over several times, for 5 minutes. This continuous stirring enables the spice mixture around the meat to come into contact with the heat at the bottom of the pot, and gives the dish its special flavour. It is known as the *bhuna* process.

8   Season with 1¼ teaspoons salt, add the puréed tomato and again stir and turn the meat. Pour in the stock, cover the pan and simmer for about 30 minutes. About 5 minutes before the meat is tender, add the turnips. Turn off the heat when the meat and turnips are tender. If the dish is not to be eaten for some time the turnips will continue to absorb some of the curry. So, when reheating, if more curry is desired just add extra water as required. Taste for seasoning, add more salt if necessary, and cook for a couple of minutes. Remove bones before serving.

This curry is deep red in colour but not as hot as it looks. If you want it hotter then increase the quantity of chilli powder.

Duck and turnips are also cooked together in the same way in Kashmir. Instead of turnips you could use potatoes and the dish would be just as nice: you do not need to salt the potatoes.

LAMB COOKED IN MILK

AAB GOSHT (KASHMIR)

This is a Kashmiri Muslim recipe. *Aab* means water in Persian, and this curry has a watery consistency. A dish with the same name, but actually a different recipe, is made by the Muslims of Bombay using coconut milk; as in kosher cooking, the Hindus do not cook meat and milk together.

This is one of the few curry recipes in which no chillies, ginger or garlic are used. It is fragrant and delicate in flavour, with a hint of sweetness. It can be fed even to a little child (in which case omit the white pepper). It is eaten with boiled rice, fragrant rice or *rotis*.

Serves 4

8 saffron strands
1½lb (700g) stewing lamb, cubed or chops
4oz (100g) shallots
4 tablespoons oil
9oz (250g) lamb bones for stock
salt
1 cinnamon or bay leaf

2 cloves
6 green cardamoms
2 1½-in (4-cm) cinnamon sticks
2 pints (1.2 litres) milk
2 tablespoons single cream
1¼ teaspoons fennel powder
½ teaspoon cumin powder
¼ teaspoon ground white pepper
½ teaspoon sugar

1   Soak the saffron strands in ¼ cup water. Soak the lamb in lukewarm water for 30 minutes, until lightened in colour.

2   Purée the peeled shallots in a food processor, or grate them, and fry in 2 tablespoons of the oil in a frying pan until golden.

3   Boil the meat and bones in a cooking pot in 6 cups water, along with ¾ teaspoon salt, the cinnamon or bay leaf, 1 clove, 3 cardamoms, 1 cinnamon stick and the fried shallots until tender. Lift out the meat and set aside. Strain the stock and discard the bones.

4   While the meat is cooking, bring the milk to boil in another pot, with the remaining clove, cardamoms and cinnamon stick. Put a wooden spoon into the pot to prevent the milk boiling over. Stir from time to time and keep cooking until the milk reduces and thickens. When it is reduced by a third, remove from the heat and leave to cool. Strain. Add the cream and stir well. Now add the meat and 3 cups of the stock to the milk.

5   Heat the remaining oil in a ladle held over a moderate heat. Add the fennel powder to the oil, then after 20 seconds add the cumin and pepper. Fry for just 10 seconds, then pour the oil mixture into the meat, add the sugar and milk; season with salt to taste. Cook for a few minutes with lid on to prevent the meat from darkening.

6   To serve, reheat uncovered and simmer for about **2** minutes. Add the saffron just before removing from the heat.

*If you require a little 'pep' in the curry you can add a couple of slit green chillies **during the last 10 minutes of the cooking time**. Remove from stock and add to the milk mixture.*

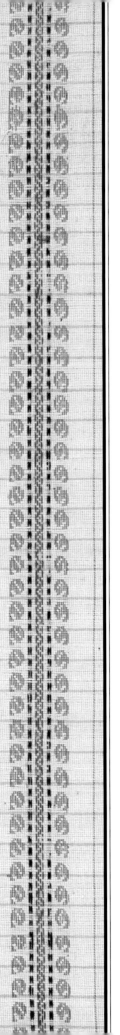

KEBAB CURRY

(KASHMIR)

This is a curry made with long kebabs of minced lamb. It is a recipe from a leading Kashmiri family, the Dhars. They call it a *kofta* curry and say that long kebabs absorb the flavour of the curry more evenly than the round ones. The *koftas* are very tender and the gravy thin but full of flavour.

The spices used are traditional in Kashmiri cooking – dried ginger (because fresh ginger was not available in Kashmir in the old days), fennel powder, large black cardamom and, of course, Kashmiri chilli powder.

This dish can be eaten with rice and/or *roti*.

Serves 6–7

For the kebabs	For the gravy
2lb (900g) very finely minced lamb	5 tablespoons full-fat yoghurt
3 teaspoons fennel powder	6 tablespoons oil
1½ teaspoons ginger powder	8 cloves
1½ teaspoons red chilli powder	2-in (5-cm) cinnamon stick
6 large black cardamoms	4 small tomatoes, chopped
1 tablespoon oil	1 tablespoon tomato paste
salt	2 tablespoons red chilli powder
1 egg	1 teaspoon ginger powder
	salt

1 To make the kebabs, mince or process the lamb once more until it is very fine.

2 Mix the fennel and ginger powders. Remove the seeds from the cardamoms and pound until crushed. Mix all the spices with the minced lamb in a bowl. Add the oil, salt to taste and the egg and mix well.

3 Keep a bowl of warm water handy to dip your hands into when making the kebabs. Take a handful of the minced meat, about the size of a lime, and roll it to a 3-inch (7.5-cm) sausage. Place on a flat dish or tray. You will get about 30 kebabs which, when cooked, will shrink to a 2-in (5-cm) length.

4 To make the gravy, whisk the yoghurt and set aside.

5 Take a cooking pot with a diameter of at least 10–12 in (25–30cm) – it can be a shallow one – into which the kebabs will fit without breaking. Heat the oil in the pot over a low heat. Add the cloves and cinnamon first, then after a minute or so add the tomatoes. Fry until the liquid from the tomatoes has almost evaporated. Stir in the tomato paste.

6 Add the chilli powder and fry for a minute, then put in the yoghurt. Stir continuously to prevent the yoghurt from curdling. Add the fennel and ginger powders, season and cook for 5 minutes, stirring all the time.

7 Add 5 cups hot water and bring to the boil. Very gently lay in the kebabs one at a time. Leave to cook for about 20 minutes over a low heat. A lot of the water will be absorbed by the kebabs. *Do not stir once the kebabs are put into the pot. If the gravy needs to be stirred, hold both sides of the pot and rock it gently.*

8 Taste and add more salt if necessary, mixing it first with water and pouring it into the pan in various places. You will know when the dish is totally ready as oil will rise to the top of the gravy.

If the kebab curry is to be reheated before serving, remove from the heat just as the oil begins to rise to the surface and set aside. Then reheat gently for 5–7 minutes, before serving.

If the mince is fatty and the curry oily, add 2 eggs instead of 1, and when the kebabs are made up, steam them for 10 minutes, allowing the fat to drip off before putting the kebabs into the pot.

LAMB CURRY WITH STIR-FRIED SPICES

BHUNA GOSHT (DELHI)

The *bhuna* process, which involves stir-frying spices in oil without adding much water, is an important part of curry-making. A curry with the name *bhuna* has a heightened flavour through prolonged frying – about 20 minutes – during which stirring must be continuous to prevent the spices from sticking to the bottom of the pot. The flavour of this dish comes from the fact that the meat cooks initially in its own juices with the spices, without any added water. The result is a wonderful curry, equally good with rice, *roti* or on sliced bread. Since a good deal of work is involved, the recipe is for 2¼lb (1kg) of lamb. Whatever is not required immediately can be frozen.

Serves 6

⅓ cup oil
3 cinnamon or bay leaves
1 black cardamom
3-in (8-cm) cinnamon stick
10 peppercorns
6 cloves
10oz (300g) onions, very finely chopped
1oz (25g) fresh ginger, puréed
⅔oz (20g) garlic, finely chopped
¼oz (8g) green chillies, chopped

2¼lb (1kg) lamb on or off the bone
   (9oz [250g] lamb bones if the meat is
   off the bone)
salt
½ teaspoon turmeric powder
1½ teaspoons coriander powder
1 teaspoon red chilli powder
1 teaspoon garam masala powder
9oz (250g) tomatoes, puréed
⅓ cup full-fat yoghurt
1 tablespoon chopped coriander leaves,
   to garnish

1 Heat the oil in a cooking pot with the cinnamon or bay leaves, cardamom and cinnamon stick. When the leaves begin to fry add the peppercorns and cloves, and after a minute put in the onions and sauté until lightly coloured, about 15 minutes.

2 Add the ginger, garlic, green chillies, lamb and bones and 1 teaspoon salt and stir-fry over a low heat for 20 minutes. During this time stir every few seconds, scraping the spices off the bottom of the pot. Add 2 tablespoons water whenever it gets too dry.

3 Then add the turmeric, coriander, red chilli and *garam masala* powders and stir continuously for 5 minutes, adding 2 tablespoons water. Add the puréed tomatoes and cook for 5 minutes, stirring frequently.

4 Add 4 cups water and simmer for 15 minutes. Lower the fire. Whisk the yoghurt and add to the pot. Cook over gentle heat until the lamb is tender. Sprinkle with chopped coriander leaves.

LAMB SHANK KORMA

NALLI KORMA (LUCKNOW)

This Lucknowi recipe is made using only lamb shanks or *nallis* as they are called in India.
It has a rich, thick gravy, not particularly spicy but aromatic with cardamom, mace,
essence of *keora* or the screwpine flower, and saffron.
The dish has a Moghul influence. Originally almonds would almost certainly have been
used instead of cashew nuts. You can use a mixture of the two, for even better effect.
The flavour and consistency of the marrow-bone stock is essential to this dish. If you wish
to use boneless meat, then make a stock with shank bones, 2 cloves garlic, 1 bay leaf and
boil for 1 hour. Strain and use instead of water to make the gravy.

Serves 4

a few strands of saffron
1 tablespoon keora or rose-water
½ cup oil
14oz (400g) onions, thinly sliced
1½oz (40g) cashew nuts (or a mixture of
  almonds and cashews)
4 green chillies, chopped
2 cinnamon or bay leaves
1 tablespoon chopped fresh ginger
1 tablespoon chopped garlic

2¼lb (1kg) lamb shanks
2 teaspoons coriander powder
1 teaspoon garam masala powder
salt
2 teaspoons red chilli powder
3 tablespoons full-fat yoghurt
¾ teaspoon mace powder
⅓ teaspoon cardamom powder (or 3 green
  cardamoms pounded with a little water)
juice of 1 lime

1   Soak the saffron strands in the *keora* or rose-water for a minimum of 15 minutes.

2   Heat half the oil in a cooking pot and fry the onions until medium-brown. Add the cashew
nuts and almonds if used and continue to fry until the onions are deep brown.

3   With a spatula extract the oil from the onions by pressing against the side of the pot. Transfer the onions and nuts to a bowl and leave to cool. Place in a blender and purée.

4   In the remaining oil sauté the green chillies, cinnamon or bay leaf, ginger, garlic, lamb,
coriander powder, and half the *garam masala* and 1½ teaspoons salt for 10 minutes, stirring
continuously. Then on a low fire add the red chilli powder and the yoghurt, stir continuously
for 3 minutes, and leave to simmer until the yoghurt is absorbed.

5   Add the fried onion purée and mix well. Put in the remaining *garam masala*, the mace and
cardamom powders and sauté for a couple of minutes. Add 4 cups water and cook until the
meat is tender. Before transferring to a serving dish, stir in the lime juice and the saffron in the
flower water.

Chops or steaks can be used instead of lamb shanks; these are much smaller in India than in
the West.

MEAT CURRY WITH CUMIN-FLAVOURED POTATOES

JEERA ALOO SALAN (LUCKNOW)

Salan is the Indian Muslim term for a curry of meat and vegetables cooked together. Meat cooked with potatoes is a popular dish all over Northern India and Pakistan. This recipe is from a gourmet Muslim family in Lucknow.

Serves 4

4 potatoes, a little bigger than an egg
salt
1 teaspoon garam masala *powder*
2 teaspoons coriander powder
1 teaspoon cumin powder
1 teaspoon red chilli powder or
* paprika*
⅓ cup oil
¾ teaspoon cumin seeds
7oz (200g) onions, thinly sliced

2 cinnamon or bay leaves
2 large black cardamoms
6 green cardamoms
¼-in (5-mm) blade of mace
2 teaspoons chopped fresh ginger
2 teaspoons chopped garlic
1½lb (700g) stewing lamb plus a couple of
* lamb bones, roughly chopped*
2-in (5-cm) cinnamon stick
6 cloves
7oz (200g) tomatoes, finely chopped

1 Rub the potatoes with a little salt and set aside for 15 minutes. Rinse and dry. Mix the 4 spice powders with 2 teaspoons water to make a paste. Reserve.

2 In a cooking pot, heat the oil and cumin seeds. When hot add the potatoes and sauté until golden and crispy. Remove the potatoes and set aside. Strain the cumin seeds from the oil and put 3 tablespoons of the strained oil back into the pot.

3 Add the onions and fry until medium-brown, stirring from time to time. Add the cinnamon or bay leaf, the seeds of the black cardamom, the whole green cardamoms and the mace. Continue to fry until the onions are deep brown, about 25 minutes in all.

4 Add the spice paste and stir-fry for a minute or two, then add 2 tablespoons water. Add the ginger and garlic and fry for another 30 seconds.

5 Now put in the lamb and bones with the cinnamon and cloves and sauté for 5–7 minutes, stirring every now and then. Add the tomatoes and let the meat fry in this mixture until the liquid from the tomato evaporates.

6 Add 3½ cups water and 1¼ teaspoons salt, cover and cook over a low heat for 35 minutes. Then put in the fried potatoes and cook until the meat is tender, making sure that the potatoes do not overcook (8–10 minutes). Remove the bones and cinnamon or bay leaf and add more salt if required. If you want more curry, then add ½ cup extra water when putting in the potatoes.

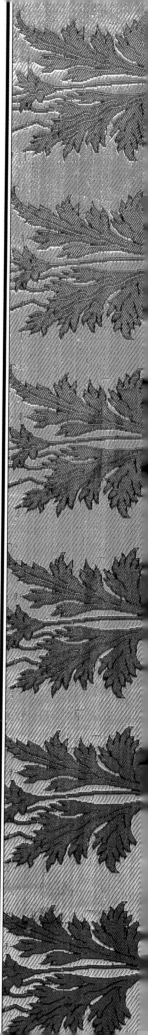

LAMB IN PICKLING SPICES

AACHAR GOSHT (BHOPAL)

Aachar is the Indian word for pickles, which are usually made using mustard oil and a special combination of spices (the same spices which are used in this dish). The curry has its origins in the courtly families of Bhopal, and first made its appearance on a menu in the Haveli restaurant at the Taj Mahal Hotel in Delhi. However, this is a homestyle recipe. The curry has a sourish tang, is greenish in colour and is not as hot as the ingredients would suggest as the chillies mellow down when braised in yoghurt. It would traditionally be made using mustard oil. However this oil has its own strong aroma and is not to everybody's taste: any other oil may be substituted. Since the green chillies are to be eaten whole, they can be de-seeded to make them milder, if liked.
It can be eaten with a *pulao* rather than a dry boiled rice, as there is little gravy, or with soft *rotis* or *parathas*.

Serves 4

1½lb (700g) stewing lamb plus a few bones or *a combination of 4 lamb chops and stewing lamb*	1 teaspoon cumin seeds
	¾ teaspoon mustard seeds
	1 teaspoon nigella seeds (kalonji)
9oz (250g) full-fat yoghurt	¾ teaspoon fenugreek seeds
1 tightly packed cup of coriander leaves with stalks	8 long, thin green chillies or Spanish chillies
9oz (250g) onions, chopped	¼ cup oil
2 teaspoons chopped garlic	a pinch of turmeric powder
1½ teaspoons chopped fresh ginger	salt
1½ teaspoons fennel seeds	

1 Soak the lamb in warm water for 15 minutes to lighten the colour. Purée the yoghurt and coriander leaves in a blender: set aside. Purée the onions, garlic and ginger in the same way.

2 Lightly pound the fennel, cumin, mustard, nigella and fenugreek seeds in a mortar with a pestle. Slit the chillies down the middle and stuff them with half the spice mixture. Reserve the remaining half.

3 In a shallow cooking pot or deep frying pan, heat the oil. Add the chillies and fry until they are pale in colour. Add the puréed onion mixture and cook for about 7–10 minutes over a moderate heat until the mixture turns pink in colour.

4 Lower the fire and add the reserved spice mixture and sauté for 1 minute, then put in the yoghurt mixture, season with the turmeric powder and 1 teaspoon salt, stirring continuously to prevent the yoghurt from curdling. Bring to the boil then add the meat (and bones, if used) and mix well. After a minute turn the heat to very low, cover with a lid and leave to cook until tender (about 45 minutes). Remove the bones before serving.

LAMB WITH SPINACH

PALAK GOSHT (PUNJAB)

Punjab is home to an earthy cuisine. The fields are full of wheat, rice, corn, mustard, tomatoes and other wonderful vegetables which the people cook well and almost always doused with home-made butter. And they love their chicken and mutton too! This is a homestyle dish, also often found in restaurants, best eaten with *parathas* or *rotis*.

Serves 4

1½lb (700g) lamb
¾ x ¼-in (2 cm x 5-mm) piece of fresh ginger
2 plump garlic cloves
1–2 green chillies
½ cup yoghurt
¼ teaspoon cumin powder
7oz (200g) spinach leaves or frozen puréed spinach
¼ cup oil
1 cinnamon or bay leaf

1 black cardamom
2 cloves
8oz (225g) onions, chopped
1 teaspoon coriander powder
½ teaspoon cumin powder
2 medium tomatoes, chopped
1 tablespoon tomato paste
1 teaspoon salt
a little nutmeg powder, to sprinkle
a knob of butter (optional)

1 Soak the lamb in warm water for 15 minutes to lighten the colour.

2 Purée the ginger, garlic and green chilli in a blender. Whisk the yoghurt and add to the ginger/garlic purée, together with the ¼ teaspoon cumin powder.

3 Marinate the lamb in this mixture for at least 1 hour, longer if possible. Meanwhile, blanch the spinach in boiling water with a little salt for 10 seconds, drain and purée the spinach.

4 Heat the oil in a cooking pot with the cinnamon or bay leaf, cardamom and cloves. When the oil is really hot and the cinnamon leaf begins to fry, add the onions. Fry for 15 minutes over a low to moderate heat.

5 Add the coriander powder and sauté for 2 minutes, stirring continuously. Add the ½ teaspoon cumin powder and after 10 seconds add a little water. Allow the spices to cook.

6 Add the meat and its marinade, stir well and cook over a moderate heat for 10 minutes, until the yoghurt is absorbed. Sauté the meat for 3 minutes, stirring continuously, then add the tomatoes and tomato paste and cook for a couple of minutes. Add 1¼ cups hot water and ¾ teaspoon of the salt. Turn the heat to low, cover with a lid and leave to simmer. When the meat is almost done, add the puréed spinach, taste for salt and mix well. Cook for 5 minutes, uncovered. When ready to serve, sprinkle with a little nutmeg powder and add a knob of butter if liked.

MEAT COOKED WITH CARDAMOM

ELAICHI GOSHT (SINDHI, FROM BOMBAY)

The Hindu Sindhis migrated from Sindh to India in 1947 (Sindh is now part of Pakistan) and the largest number of them settled in Bombay. Sindhi food is not found outside Sindhi homes. This is my mother's recipe and is extremely simple to make, involving just a few ingredients.

A very delicate mutton dish with a thin gravy full of the flavour of cardamom (*elaichi*) and black pepper, this is a favourite of the Sindhis. Dishes with pepper seem to be a standard prescription in many parts of India for women after childbirth, and in the region around Hyderabad town in Sindh this dish was given *every day* to new mothers. It is traditionally eaten with *chapatis* though it can equally well be eaten with rice.

Serves 6

2¼lb (1kg) lamb, on or off the bone
½ cup full-fat yoghurt
35 green cardamoms
½ cup oil
2 teaspoons ground black pepper
1 teaspoon turmeric powder

1 teaspoon chilli powder
2 teaspoons coriander powder
3 medium tomatoes (sourish variety),
 finely chopped
salt

1 If the lamb is on the bone, wash it in warm water. Whisk the yoghurt with a fork in a bowl.

2 Grind the whole green cardamoms in a blender with a little water, or dry in a coffee grinder and then mix with a little water to make a paste.

3 Heat the oil in a cooking pot. Add the cardamom paste and the pepper and fry over a low heat for 2–3 minutes. Add the meat, turmeric, chilli and coriander powders and sauté for 10 minutes, stirring all the time to prevent the mixture from sticking to the bottom of the pot, adding water if necessary.

4 Lower the fire and add the yoghurt, tomatoes and salt to taste and continue to sauté for a further 5 minutes. Add about 4 cups water, cover the pot and leave to simmer over a low heat until the meat is tender.

The secret of success with this dish lies in making sure that the meat and spices are fried for a full 10 minutes (step 3) without allowing the spices to burn. Therefore it is essential to keep the heat low and use the recommended amount of oil.

LAMB SLOW-COOKED IN ONIONS & YOGHURT

SEYAL GOSHT (SINDHI, FROM BOMBAY)

Seyal in the Sindhi language means cooking in onions and herbs without adding any
water. Lamb (or, in India, mutton) is braised in lots of chopped onions, tomato and
yoghurt and flavoured with whole and ground spices and herbs. It has a wholesome taste
and makes a nice family dish. The curry has a thick-textured gravy.
It is eaten with *rotis* or may be heaped on slices of bread because of the thick onion gravy.
Perfect this way for a brunch, Sunday lunch or high tea. If you want to eat it with rice,
then make a *pulao*.

Serves 6

1¾lb (850g) large onions, chopped
1lb (450g) tomatoes
1½ cups full-fat yoghurt
2 cups coriander leaves
3 green chillies
2¼lb (1kg) mixture of stewing
  lamb and lamb chops
4 cinnamon or bay leaves
2 large black cardamoms
6 green cardamoms
1 blade of mace
2-in (5-cm) cinnamon stick
12 peppercorns

6 cloves
⅔ cup oil
6 teaspoons chopped fresh ginger
6 teaspoons chopped garlic
4½ teaspoons coriander powder
2 teaspoons cumin powder
½ teaspoon turmeric powder
2 teaspoons red chilli powder
  (or paprika for a milder result)
1 teaspoon caraway seeds
1 teaspoon green cardamom
  powder
salt

1 Purée the onions in a blender and place in a bowl. In the same blender purée the tomatoes and transfer to another bowl.

2 Again in the blender, purée the yoghurt, coriander leaves and green chillies. Marinate the lamb in this mixture for at least 1 hour.

3 Make a bouquet garni by tying up the cinnamon or bay leaves, black and green cardamoms, mace, cinnamon, peppercorns and cloves in a small piece of cheesecloth. (In India the spices are put directly into the cooking pot and you can do so if you do not mind avoiding them while eating. If so, you need not make the bouquet garni.)

4 Heat half the oil in a cooking pot, then add the onion purée and cook over a moderate heat for 20 minutes so that some of the moisture evaporates. Stir from time to time.

5 Meanwhile, put the remaining oil with the bouquet garni or whole spices in a frying pan over a low heat. After 2 minutes add the ginger and garlic, followed 2 minutes later by the coriander, cumin, turmeric and red chilli powders together with 3 tablespoons water. Stir well to blend with the oil. Sauté for 2 minutes, then pour into the onion mixture.

6 Add the puréed tomato and sauté for about 5 minutes. Leave to cool, then add the meat and yoghurt and marinate for 1 further hour.

7 Add 2 teaspoons salt and mix well. Cook over a high heat for 5 minutes so that the meat juices are sealed. Now turn the fire to low and gently cook until the meat is tender; or you can transfer it to an earthenware dish and cook in an oven pre-heated to 160°C/325°F/Gas Mark 3 for 1½ hours. Before serving, discard the bouquet garni, pound the caraway seeds and sprinkle them over with the cardamom powder for a wonderful aroma.

Since there is no opportunity to use stock in this recipe, it is advisable to use at least some meat on the bone. It is not essential that it should include lamb chops. You can select some other pieces. But if using only stewing lamb then put in at least 2 medium-sized pieces of bone during cooking, and remove before serving.

LAMB WITH APRICOTS

JARDALOO BOTI (BOMBAY)

Lamb or chicken with apricots is a popular Parsee dish, and the Persian influence shows because it is the Hunza or Afghani apricots that are used. These are the best ones to use but those found in supermarkets can be substituted.

This is quite a simple dish to prepare, and has a tinge of sweet and sour. It is best with a yellow-coloured rice but can also be eaten just with side vegetables, as in Western cuisine.

Serves 4

4oz (100g) dried Hunza apricots
¼ cup oil
2 onions, very finely chopped
½-in (1-cm) square piece of fresh ginger, chopped
2 plump garlic cloves, finely chopped
3-in (7.5-cm) cinnamon stick
6 green cardamoms

1½ teaspoons red chilli powder
½ teaspoon cumin powder
2 tomatoes, chopped
1½lb (700g) stewing lamb
¾ teaspoon garam masala powder
¼ teaspoon ground black pepper
salt
1 teaspoon plus a few drops of wine vinegar
1 teaspoon sugar

1 Soak the apricots in 1 cup water, with half a teaspoon of vinegar added, for 3 hours. Remove the stones.

2 Heat the oil in a cooking pot and fry the onions for about 12 minutes until golden-brown. Add the ginger and garlic. After 3 minutes add the cinnamon and cardamoms. After a further minute add the chilli and cumin powders, and stir well.

3 Add the tomatoes and cook for 5 minutes. Then add the meat, *garam masala* powder and pepper and stir-fry in the spices for about 5 minutes. Add salt to taste, together with 1 cup water, then cook slowly over a very low heat until tender. If all the liquid evaporates, add ½ cup water.

4 When the meat is done, add 1 teaspoon vinegar, the sugar and the drained apricots, and cook for a further 10 minutes, mixing well. Serve.

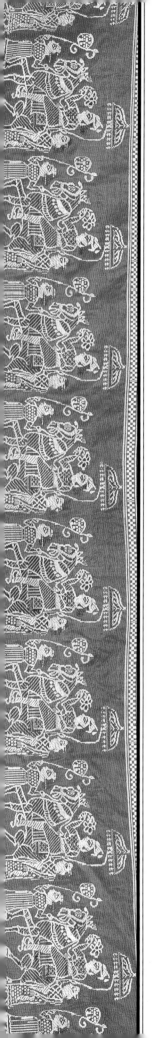

BORI CURRY

KAARI (BOMBAY)

The Boris are a Muslim trading community originally from Gujarat but now living only in Bombay and a few places in Gujarat like Surat. Their cuisine is well liked by the people of Bombay and certain dishes, like *biryani* and *khichda* (a wheat, meat and lentil porridge) are relished by everyone. This curry is not well known as it is not available in any restaurant. It is called a *kaari* and the Aga Khanis, also a Muslim community, call it a Curry Chawal (*chawal* meaning rice, so curry and rice). They buy a ready-mixed curry powder from grocers of their own community, and this contains the powdered peanuts and grams (*chanas*). The recipe given here enables you to make this delicious curry without resorting to the commercial powder.

Meat and potatoes are cooked together and the dish has a golden colour, creamy texture and a mild taste which blends the Moghul richness of nuts with the flavours of Bombay – coconut, sesame seeds and curry leaves.

Serves 4

10 almonds	9oz (250g) medium potatoes
8 cashew nuts	⅓ cup oil
1 tablespoon roasted peanuts	5 cloves
1 tablespoon roasted gram	6-in (15-cm) cinnamon stick
2 teaspoons sesame seeds	15 curry leaves
1 onion, chopped	salt
4 heaped teaspoons coriander seeds	9oz (250g) small onions, sliced
2 teaspoons cumin seeds	1½lb (700g) stewing lamb and a few
12 dried whole red chillies	bones for stock
6 teaspoons dessicated coconut	½ teaspoon turmeric powder
2½oz (70g) fresh coconut, sliced	½ teaspoon garam masala powder
1oz (25g) tamarind pulp	3 green chillies
	½ cup coriander leaves, chopped
	1 tablespoon mint leaves, chopped

1 To prepare the spice mixture, put the almonds, cashew nuts, peanuts, gram, sesame seeds and the onion in a pan or on a griddle and heat for about 5 minutes. Remove and set aside. Now put in the coriander seeds, cumin seeds, dried red chillies and coconut, and heat for just 2 minutes (because the griddle will be hot already). Put all the nuts and spices into a blender, add ½ cup water and grind to a paste.

2 Cut the fresh coconut into pieces. Put into a blender with 2 cups water and liquidize. Strain the liquid and set aside.

3 Soak the tamarind pulp in ½ cup water. Peel the potatoes and cut into half crossways, or if using large potatoes, cut into quarters.

4 Heat the oil in a cooking pot and when hot add the cloves, cinnamon, peppercorns and half the curry leaves and fry over a low heat for 2 minutes. Add the potatoes and a little salt and fry for 5 minutes. Remove the potatoes and set aside.

5 Add the sliced onions to the pot and fry for 7–8 minutes. Add the meat and fry for 5 minutes, then add the remaining curry leaves. Add 3 cups water and salt to taste and cook for about 40 minutes over a low heat.

6 Add the nut and spice paste, the turmeric and *garam masala* powders, and the chillies. Add the tamarind water and stir.

7 Add the potatoes, the coconut milk, the coriander leaves and mint leaves and cook covered for 30 minutes or until the meat is tender. Remove from the heat and keep covered until ready to serve.

Besan flour is made from roasted gram flour, so if grams are difficult to get, you should be able to buy besan from an Indian grocer. Put a tablespoon of gram flour into the spice mixture when grinding, instead of roasted grams.

MUTTON CURRY

ANDHRA STYLE (NELLORE IN ANDHRA)

Andhra cuisine is the spiciest and hottest cuisine in India, and the chilli powder used is the hottest variety – from Guntur. However, the cooling quality of the yoghurt balances the heat of the chilli powder in this recipe, which is from the home of Mr Chenna Reddy, a former Chief Minister of Andhra, who keeps an excellent table. Mrs Reddy supervises all the cooking, and this is her recipe. I have reduced the garlic and ginger by half a teaspoon each, as the full quantity can be overpowering for some.

This curry should be eaten with rice, or if made a little thicker by adding less water, is equally delicious with *rotis*.

Serves 4

¾ cup full-fat yoghurt
2½ teaspoons garlic purée
2½ teaspoons ginger purée
2 teaspoons red chilli powder
½ teaspoon turmeric powder
2 tablespoons chopped coriander leaves
1½lb (700g) stewing lamb
3 tablespoons oil

2 medium onions, finely chopped
2 green cardamoms
4 cloves
3 medium tomatoes, finely chopped
½ teaspoon caraway seeds
10–12 curry leaves
4 green cardamoms
salt

1 Whisk the yoghurt well and add the garlic and ginger purée, the chilli and turmeric powders and the coriander leaves. Mix well. Marinate the meat in this mixture for 2–4 hours. If it is warm, then put the meat into the refrigerator.

2 Heat the oil in a cooking pot and fry the onions until medium-brown. Add the cardamoms and cloves and fry for 1 minute.

3 Add the meat with the marinade and after 5 minutes turn the heat to very low. Cook for about 10 minutes until the marinade is absorbed. Then sauté or *bhuna* the meat, stirring continuously for about 5 minutes.

4 Now add the tomatoes and cook for 5 minutes until the liquid is absorbed. Then *bhuna* again for 5 minutes.

5 Add the caraway seeds, curry leaves and salt to taste and stir for 2 minutes. Then add 3–4 cups hot water (depending on the consistency of gravy required) and leave to cook, covered, over a low heat, until the meat is tender.

You can add potatoes to this curry if you wish, in which case, peel and cut 2 medium-sized potatoes into quarters and put into the mixture 20 minutes before it is ready. Or use 6–8 small potatoes. Increase the water to be added by ¾ cups and add a pinch of extra salt.

MINCED LAMB WITH CORIANDER

DHANIYA KEEMA (HYDERABAD)

It is not the done thing to serve minced meat to guests in the West, but minced mutton is a delicacy among Indian Muslims and they make it really well. So, it would be a pity not to include a recipe for it. In Hyderabad they have a version with fresh coriander leaves. The secret is to use lean lamb for the mince, and to have it minced extremely fine. Serve with *roti*, bread, rice or as part of a Western-type meal, together with side vegetables. It goes well with pasta, too.

Serves 4

1½lb (700g) finely minced lamb
3 garlic cloves
2 cinnamon or bay leaves
⅓ cup oil
10oz (300g) onions, finely chopped
2-in (5-cm) cinnamon stick
3 cloves
3 green cardamoms
½ x ¼-in (1-cm x 5-mm) piece of fresh
 ginger, finely chopped

1–2 green chillies, finely chopped
¼ teaspoon turmeric powder
¾ teaspoon cumin powder
1 teaspoon coriander powder
1 teaspoon garam masala *powder*
2 tomatoes, finely chopped
salt
1 cup coriander leaves, finely chopped

1 Boil the mince in 2 cups water, with 1 whole peeled garlic clove and the cinnamon or bay leaves, for 10 minutes. Strain away the water. This will remove the odour of the mince.

2 Finely chop the remaining garlic cloves.

3 Heat the oil in a cooking pot. Fry the onions until golden-brown (about 20 minutes). Add the cinnamon, cloves, cardamoms, ginger, garlic and chillies. Cook for 2 minutes, then add the mince and sauté for 5 minutes. Add the turmeric, cumin and half the *garam masala* powder and sauté for a further 5 minutes, stirring every minute or so. Add the tomato and salt to taste.

4 When the tomato is totally absorbed, stir-fry for 2 minutes or so. Add 2 cups water and cook until tender. When done, add the coriander leaves and remaining *garam masala*. Stir well and cook for 3 minutes or so, uncovered. This dish has very little gravy.

MEAT WITH LENTILS

DALCHA (HYDERABAD)

Cooking lamb or mutton with lentils is popular in Northern and Western India. The North Indians make *daal gosht*, the Parsees in the West make *dhansak*, the Boris of Bombay make *khichda* and the Hyderabadi Muslims make *haleem* and *dalcha*. *Dalcha* has a sourish tang with herbal overtones of curry leaves and fresh coriander.

Serves 8

a few lamb bones
1 bay leaf
1 garlic clove
9oz (250g) gram dal *(chana dal)*
9oz (250g) toor dal
2oz (50g) tamarind
salt
¾ teaspoon turmeric powder
6 green chillies, chopped
3 tablespoons coriander leaves, chopped
25 curry leaves
8 tablespoons oil
9oz (250g) onions, sliced

6 cloves
6 green cardamoms
4-in (10-cm) cinnamon stick
2 teaspoons red chilli powder
3 teaspoons garlic purée
3 teaspoons ginger purée
1½lb (700g) stewing lamb
3 tomatoes, chopped

For seasoning
6 dried red chillies (optional)
3 garlic cloves, crushed
1 teaspoon cumin seeds
¼ teaspoon mustard seeds
⅓ teaspoon garam masala *powder*

1 Put the lamb bones to boil in 5 cups water with the bay leaf and garlic clove for 30 minutes. Skim off the scum. Strain the stock and set aside.

2 Wash both *dals* and soak them separately for 4 hours. Soak the tamarind in 1 cup water for 1 hour, then press out the juice, strain and set aside the tamarind water.

3 Put both *dals* into a cooking pot with 8 cups water and 1 teaspoon salt, the turmeric powder, 3 of the green chillies, 1 tablespoon of the coriander leaves and 10 of the curry leaves. Cook for 1½ hours or until tender. Liquidize to a creamy consistency.

4 Heat half the oil in another large cooking pot and sauté the onions for 5–7 minutes. Then add the cloves, cardamoms, cinnamon, the remaining green chillies, the red chilli powder, the remaining coriander and 10 of the curry leaves and the garlic and ginger purée. Stir to prevent the spices from sticking to the pot. Sprinkle over 2 tablespoons water if necessary.

5 Add the lamb and sauté over a moderate heat for 5 minutes. Add the tomato and sauté for a further 5 minutes. Stir in the puréed *dals* and the stock, adding water to total 4 cups. Add salt to taste (about ¾ teaspoon) and leave to cook, covered, over a moderate heat until the lamb is tender. This should take about 50–60 minutes. Then add the tamarind water and remaining curry leaves and simmer for a couple of minutes.

6 Just before serving, season by heating the remaining oil in a large ladle or small frying pan and frying the red chillies broken into two, if used, the garlic, cumin seeds, mustard seeds and *garam masala* powder (in this order). Fry for 10 seconds after the addition of the last ingredient. Add this seasoning to the curry and stir. It is now ready to serve.

LAMB CURRY

MADRAS STYLE (TAMIL NADU)

The standard Madras curry in restaurants in the UK is not to be found anywhere in
Madras! However, once when I was travelling into the deep south of the Coromandel
coast of India, near the seventeenth-century Danish settlement of Tranquebar, it was
lunch-time and there was no eatery in sight. The local village cook made a stunning
mutton curry, reproduced here using lamb.
Easy to make, it is perfect for a get-together with family or friends.

Serves 6

4oz (120g) fresh coconut
8–12 whole red chillies, dried
3 teaspoons paprika powder
1 x ½-in (2.5 x 1-cm) piece of fresh
 ginger
6 plump garlic cloves
3 teaspoons coriander powder
4 peppercorns
2 cinnamon or bay leaves
4-in (10-cm) cinnamon stick

6 cloves
1 teaspoon cumin seeds
1 teaspoon poppy seeds
½ teaspoon fennel seeds
3 tablespoons oil
2 large onions, chopped
2¼lb (1kg) stewing lamb
3 tomatoes, chopped
salt

1 Cut half the coconut into small pieces for grinding with spices and set aside. Cut the remain-
der into pieces and put into a blender with 2 cups warm water. Blend until smooth, then strain
and reserve the coconut milk.

2 Grind together the chopped coconut, chillies and the ginger, garlic and all the spices to make
a smooth paste, adding a little water.

3 Heat the oil in a cooking pot and fry the onions until brown. Add the spice paste and fry for
about 15 minutes over a low heat, stirring in 3 tablespoons water in the process.

4 Add the meat and sauté for 5 minutes over a moderate heat. Add the tomatoes and sauté for
a further 5 minutes. Add salt to taste.

5 Add 4 cups warm water and cook, covered, until the meat is done (about 50–60 minutes).
Then add the coconut milk and simmer for a few minutes before serving.

WHITE CHICKEN KORMA

SAFED MURGH KORMA (AGRA)

A mild aromatic *korma*, this is basically a Muslim court dish, a blend of Moghlai and Nawabi cuisine. The Moghul Emperor Shahjehan, builder of the Taj Mahal monument, used to have all-white banquets on full moon nights at the Agra Fort. The terrace of the fort was bedecked with white carpets and cushions and white flowers, the guests dressed in white, and all the dishes served were white in colour. The white *korma* was later perfected at the tables of the gourmet Nawabs of Oudh in Lucknow. The Royal House of Jaipur, connected by marriage to the Moghuls, also served all-white banquets on the night of Sharad Poornima, the September full moon, as late as the 1960s.
Originally this dish was made with almonds only, but modern cooks prefer a combination of cashews and almonds. The traditional Lucknowi recipe also includes 1oz (25g) *chaar magaz* or 'four seeds', a mix of various melon, squash and pumpkin seeds available in India from speciality grocers, and a teaspoon of powdered rose petals, but these are omitted here.

Serves 4

1½ teaspoons poppy seeds
5oz (150g) full-fat yoghurt
⅓ cup ghee *or clarified butter*
2oz (50g) blanched almonds
2oz (50g) unsalted cashew nuts
2 cinnamon leaves or bay leaves
12oz (350g) onions, chopped
3 green chillies, chopped

4 green cardamoms
2 teaspoons finely chopped garlic
2 teaspoons finely chopped fresh ginger
1 whole green chilli
1 clove
2¼lb (1kg) boneless chicken breasts, skinned
½ teaspoon nutmeg powder
½ teaspoon mace powder
salt

1 Soak the poppy seeds in ½ cup water for 1 hour. Then drain off the water and grind into a fine paste with a pestle and mortar.

2 Hang the yoghurt in a cheese-cloth for 1 hour to drain off the whey. Then put the hung yoghurt into a bowl and whisk.

3 Heat most of the *ghee* or clarified butter in a cooking pot, add the almonds, cashews and cinnamon or bay leaf and fry for about 7–8 minutes over a moderate heat. Add the onions and fry for about 10 minutes or until lightly coloured. Add the chopped green chillies, cardamoms and ground poppy seeds and fry for about 3–4 minutes. Add 1 cup water and cook for 10 minutes. Remove from the heat, discard the cinnamon or bay leaf and leave to cool. Put the mixture into a blender and purée to a smooth paste without any grains.

4 Add 1 tablespoon *ghee* or clarified butter to the cooking pot, then add the garlic, ginger, whole green chilli and clove. After 1 minute add the chicken pieces. The chicken will gradually release its juices until the meat is almost dry. Then add the yoghurt and stir continuously to prevent it from curdling.

5 Add the ground spice mixture with the nutmeg and mace powders and salt to taste. Stir well and add 1½ cups hot water. Taste the mixture. If you find it bland, you can add additional whole green chillies. Cook over a low heat for about 30 minutes until the chicken is tender.

CHICKEN KORMA WITH CORIANDER LEAVES

DHANIWALI MURGH KORMA (KASHMIR)

Kashmir is actually sheep and goat country and chicken is eaten rarely. This recipe was shown to me by Abdul Ahad Waza who is the premier Kashmir wedding and party caterer. Along with his four sons he cooks in his courtyard and supplies food to the culinary cognoscenti of Kashmir and in the winter does the same in Delhi. This is rather an unusual-flavoured Chicken Korma, mild and fragrant with a thin gravy. Good to eat with rice, *roti* or even sliced bread.

Serves 4

2¼lb (1kg) chicken
5 garlic cloves
10–12 strands of saffron
2 onions, chopped
5 green chillies, chopped
1½ cups full-fat yoghurt
¼ cup ghee *or oil*
4 cloves

8 green cardamoms
4-in (10-cm) cinnamon stick
½ teaspoon turmeric powder
½ teaspoon ginger powder
salt
2 cups chicken stock
¼ teaspoon ground black pepper
2 tablespoons chopped coriander leaves

1 Boil the chicken in 3 cups water along with 2 of the garlic cloves for 3–4 minutes. Strain and discard water. Leave the chicken to cool, then rinse in lukewarm water. This removes all the odour of the chicken. Cut up the chicken.

2 Pound the remaining garlic and soak in ½ cup water to obtain a garlic infusion. Soak the saffron strands in ¼ cup water, pressing with the back of a spoon to get an infusion. Purée the onions with the green chillies. Whisk the yoghurt and set aside.

3 Heat the *ghee* or oil in a cooking pot and fry the onion purée until golden (about 12–15 minutes). Add the cloves, cardamoms and cinnamon followed by the turmeric powder. Add the chicken, garlic infusion and yoghurt and cover with a lid. Allow to simmer for 7–10 minutes until the juices are absorbed.

4 Add the ginger powder and salt to taste and sauté for 3–4 minutes until the chicken is lightly browned. Add enough chicken stock to get the amount of gravy desired (this dish does not need a great deal).

5 Simmer for 40 minutes over a gentle heat. When the chicken is tender, sprinkle with the saffron infusion, pepper and fresh coriander leaves.

BUTTER CHICKEN

MURGH MAKHANI (DELHI)

Chicken Makhani, made either with *tikkas* – derived from the Hindi word *tukra* and meaning pieces – or quarters of chicken, is the most popular dish in Indian restaurants both in India and overseas. It is essentially a restaurant and not a homestyle dish, because there are no *tandoors* in Indian home kitchens, and this dish consists of *tandoor*-cooked chicken in a sauce.

However, since the dish is so popular, many would like to recreate it at home, and I give a simplified way to do so here, cooking the chicken in a skillet. Alternatively, it is possible to roast a whole small chicken, marinating it first then quartering it and adding the juices from the roasting pan into the *makhani* sauce.

Butter chicken originated in the 1950s at the Moti Mahal restaurant in Delhi where they made the sauce by adding butter and tomato to the leftover chicken juices in the marinade trays from which they used to sell hundreds of portions of Tandoori Chicken every day.

Serves 4

2lb (900g) chicken (skinned quarters, smaller
   pieces on the bone) or boneless pieces (tikkas)
4–5 tablespoons oil

For the marinade
2 cups full-fat yoghurt
6 garlic cloves
½-in (1-cm) square of fresh ginger
⅔ teaspoon red chilli powder or paprika
¼ teaspoon coriander powder
½ teaspoon cumin powder
½ teaspoon garam masala powder
a tiny pinch of tandoori colouring (optional)
½ teaspoon salt
2 teaspoons lime juice

For the mahkani sauce
1½lb (700g) tomatoes
½ teaspoon kasuri methi
   (dried fenugreek leaves)
3oz (75g) chilled butter
½ teaspoon paprika
few drops of vinegar
¼ teaspoon garam masala powder
salt
1½ oz (40g) single cream

1 First prepare the marinade. Place the yoghurt in a piece of cheesecloth and leave to hang to allow the whey to drip away. Purée the garlic and ginger in a blender. Add this and the marinade spices, salt and lime juice to the yoghurt and mix well.

2 Scald the tomatoes for the *makhani* sauce and peel off the skin. Reduce to a semi-pulp with a fork or potato masher. Put the *kasuri methi* into a grinder and reduce to a powder.

3 Make gashes in the chicken if using pieces on the bone. Marinate the chicken in the yoghurt mixture for at least 1 hour, preferably 2; for best results leave overnight.

4 When ready to cook, heat the oil in a large, thick-bottomed skillet and put in the chicken with the marinade. Cover and cook over a low heat until done. Turn the chicken over during cooking.

5 Put the tomato pulp into a frying pan and cook for 5 minutes or so until the liquid has evaporated slightly.

6 Add the chilled butter and paprika; after the butter has melted, let it cook for just 1 minute. Taste. If it has no sourness, add a few drops of vinegar. Add the *kasuri methi* and *garam masala* powder and salt to taste. After 30 seconds, add the cream and stir. The sauce is now ready. Pour it into the skillet and mix well with the chicken. Serve immediately.

If butter is cooked for as long as 3 minutes it will turn into ghee and become a grainy emulsion. So start with chilled butter and cook for less than 2 minutes after the butter has melted.

You can cook the chicken ahead of time. But makhani sauce takes only 5–6 minutes to prepare and should be made when the dish is to be eaten. You can cook the tomato ahead, but add the butter just before serving.

In India, restaurateurs mix a little raw papaya purée into the marinade as a tenderizer.

CHICKEN PISTACHIO KORMA

PISTA CHICKEN (DELHI)

I first ate this dish long ago in a small roadside restaurant in a by-lane in the heart of Bombay's bazaar areas. Years later I met the cook, who originally comes from a family of professional wedding caterers near the Jama Masjid mosque area of Old Delhi.

It is very delicate in taste, and attractive to look at with its creamy light green colour. The taste depends on the quality of pistachios used – the brighter green, the better. This dish deserves all-white meat, so breast of chicken is best. One can of course make it with a whole chicken as well.

Serves 4

2¼lb (1kg) chicken
4oz (100g) shelled pistachio nuts, unsalted
8 green chillies
5 tablespoons single cream
3 tablespoons full-fat yoghurt
2 onions, chopped
oil
1 x ½-in (2.5 x 1-cm) piece of fresh ginger, chopped

6 plump garlic cloves
¾ teaspoon garam masala *powder*
⅛ teaspoon turmeric powder
2 cinnamon or bay leaves
¾ teaspoon ground white pepper
1¼ teaspoons fennel seeds
1 tomato, chopped
salt
1 teaspoon green cardamom powder
2 tablespoons chopped coriander leaves

1 Cut the chicken into pieces as desired. Use the bones and trimmings to make 3 cups stock.

2 Boil the pistachios for 10 minutes in 1 cup water. Remove from the heat, drain and leave to cool. Rub the nuts with your fingers to remove the skin. Grind the pistachios with 4 of the green chillies and cream and reduce to a paste in a blender.

3 Whisk the yoghurt well with a fork.

4 Fry the onions in the oil in a cooking pot until lightly coloured. Add the ginger, garlic, *garam masala* and turmeric powders, cinnamon or bay leaves, white pepper and fennel seeds and fry for 2 minutes. Add the pistachio mixture and fry for 2 minutes.

5 Add the chicken and sauté for 5 minutes. Then add the tomato, yoghurt, remaining chillies and salt to taste. Add the chicken stock (or water) and cook until done, about 15–20 minutes depending on the size of chicken pieces. Sprinkle with cardamom powder and coriander leaves just before serving.

In India, gourmets use Peshwari pistachios for their taste and bright green colour.

CHICKEN AND CASHEW NUTS IN BLACK SPICES

KAJU CHICKEN IN KAALA MASALA (BOMBAY)

Maharashtrians have a powdered spice mixture called *kaala masala* which they use in many dishes. *Kaala* means black, and it is a combination of dark-coloured spices, a kind of *garam masala* with the addition of coriander seeds and cumin.
This is a thick, nutty curry of chicken with lots of cashew nuts, whole and crushed, and is delicious. The recipe comes from the wife of the famous gynaecologist of Bombay, the late Dr Shirodkar. Eat it with *rotis*. Lemon rice (without the cashew nuts) also goes well with it since the dish has no touch of sourness.

Serves 4

2¼lb (1kg) chicken, skinned
4oz (100g) grated coconut
12 plump garlic cloves, peeled
1 x ½-in (2.5 x 1-cm) piece of fresh
 ginger, chopped
2½ tablespoons coriander seeds

1½ teaspoons cumin seeds
6 whole dried red chillies
6 cloves
3-in (7.5-cm) cinnamon stick
8oz (225g) cashew nuts
1 large onion, chopped
5 tablespoons oil
salt

1 Cut the chicken into 8 pieces.

2 In a large frying pan, without any fat or oil, roast the coconut, garlic, ginger, coriander seeds, cumin seeds, red chillies, cloves and cinnamon over a low heat. After 5 minutes add 2oz (50g) of the cashew nuts and the onion and roast for a further 10 minutes, stirring all the time. Turn off the heat and leave to cool. Grind the mixture in a blender or food processor with ¾ cup water to a fine consistency.

3 Separately grind 1oz (25g) of the remaining cashew nuts with a little water to make a fine paste and set aside.

4 Heat the oil in a cooking pot, add the ground spice mixture and fry for 10 minutes over a low heat. Add the ground cashew nuts and salt to taste and fry for a further 2–3 minutes.

5 Add the chicken, turn up the heat to moderate and fry for 5 minutes. Then add 3 cups water and leave to cook over a low heat for 10 minutes, covered.

6 Add the remaining cashew nuts and continue to cook until the chicken is done. You should have a thick, dark curry with whole cashew nuts in it.

When grinding the spices and cashew nuts make sure that the resultant paste is smooth and fine by grinding for a long time until you get this consistency. If not, the curry will look as if it has curdled.

CHICKEN COOKED WITH LENTILS AND VEGETABLES

DHANSAK (BOMBAY)

Dhansak is the best-known and liked dish in Parsee cuisine. The Parsees fled from Persia to avoid religious persecution in the thirteenth century and settled on the Western Coast of India, in what is now Gujarat State. They adopted Gujarati as their language and absorbed local influences into their cuisine. *Dhan* in Gujarati means wealth, but in Parsee Gujarati *Dhaan* means rice. *Sak* means vegetables. *Dhansak* is a meat, vegetable and lentil curry eaten with a caramelized brown *pulao* rice. It is often eaten at Sunday lunch but is not served on auspicious occasions since it is customarily eaten on the fourth day after a funeral. Although there are many ingredients, it is quite simple to prepare. The *dhansak masala* may be available in some Indian grocers, but Parsee *sambar masala* has not yet found its way to the West.

Serves 6

3lb (1.4kg) chicken, cut into 6 or more pieces	*salt*
10oz (300g) toor dal *(whole dried variety)*	*½ cup oil*
2oz (50g) tamarind pulp	*½ bunch fresh fenugreek or 2 teaspoons*
2in (5cm) square piece of fresh ginger	*dried fenugreek leaves* (kasuri methi)
6 garlic cloves	*3 teaspoons Parsee* sambar masala
2 large onions, chopped	*2 teaspoons* dhansak masala
7oz (200g) red pumpkin, chopped	*1 teaspoon cumin powder*
5oz (150g) aubergines, chopped	*3 teaspoons coriander powder*
1 potato, chopped	*2 teaspoons red chilli powder*
¼ cup fresh dill, finely chopped	*3 tomatoes, chopped*
½ teaspoon turmeric powder	*6 green chillies, chopped*
1 cup + 1 tablespoon coriander leaves	*1 tablespoon jaggery or palm sugar*
20 leaves fresh mint	*juice of 1 lime*

1 Make a chicken stock with the bones, neck, giblets and trimmings.

2 Wash the *toor dal* and soak it in water for 30 minutes. Soak the tamarind in 1 cup water for at least 30 minutes.

3 Chop 1½-in (4-cm) piece of the ginger and 4 of the garlic cloves.

4 In a large cooking pot, put the *dal* to cook in 3 cups water along with the onions, pumpkin, aubergines, potato and dill. Add the turmeric, whole remaining piece of ginger, remaining 2 garlic cloves, 1 tablespoon of the coriander leaves and 8 of the mint leaves. Simmer until the *dal* is very soft. Allow to cool slightly. Liquidize with an egg-beater to achieve a creamy consistency. Season with 1 teaspoon salt.

5 While the *dal* is cooking, heat the oil in a large frying pan and fry the chopped ginger, garlic, 1 cup coriander leaves, 12 mint leaves, fenugreek, *sambar masala, dhansak masala,* cumin and coriander powders, tomatoes and green chillies and fry for 2 minutes, stirring continuously. Add the chicken and sauté for 2 minutes. Season with 1 teaspoon salt and stir well.

6 Add the chicken to the *dal* with 3 cups chicken stock or water. Add the *jaggery.* Simmer until the chicken is cooked through before adding the tamarind water and lime juice; adjust for salt, then simmer for a couple of minutes. It is now ready to serve.

This is a straightforward and tasty recipe for dhansak. *Parsees who are fastidious use a mix of dals – 7oz (200g) of toor dal and 1 tablespoon each of moong, masoor and val dal.*

Dhansak *powder in packet form is available at Indian grocers. If unavailable use 1½ teaspoons garam masala and ½ teaspoon star anise powder and ¼ teaspoon nutmeg powder.*

Instead of Parsee sambar masala *make the following mix: ¾ teaspoon fenugreek powder, ½ teaspoon mustard powder, 1 teaspoon red chilli powder and ½ teaspoon ground pepper.*

CHICKEN IN THICK COCONUT GRAVY

KORI GASHI (MANGALORE)

Mangalore is a port town just off Goa on the West coast of India. The cuisine of Mangalore features a lot of seafood and also includes chicken, unlike Goa where chicken is eaten rarely. The Hindus and Christians both have interesting curries. The *Gashi* is a thick coconut gravy with a grainy texture.

This recipe is from a Hindu family. It is reddish-brown in colour and slightly on the hot side. The exact degree of spiciness depends on the variety of chilli used. In Mangalore the *bedgi* chilli is used, which looks like the Kashmiri chilli but is more pungent – with lots of colour. It is different from other coconut and chilli-based curries in that the coconut and spices are fried in oil *before* grinding, and there are a few unusual spices for this kind of curry – mustard seeds and fenugreek seeds. The tamarind is also ground with the spices. The fresh curry leaves give *Kori Gashi* a distinctive aroma.

Serves 4–5

2 cups grated fresh coconut	1 teaspoon cumin seeds
1 x ½-in (2.5 x 1-cm) piece of	8 peppercorns
fresh ginger	4 cloves
5 plump garlic cloves	½ teaspoon turmeric powder
5 tablespoons oil	1oz (25g) tamarind pulp
15 whole dried red chillies	2 cups chopped onion
4 heaped teaspoons coriander seeds	10–12 curry leaves
¼ teaspoon mustard seeds	salt
½ teaspoon fenugreek seeds	2¼lb (1kg) chicken pieces, on or off
2-in (5-cm) cinnamon stick	the bone, skinned

1 Soak half the grated coconut in 1 cup warm water for 30 minutes, then put it into a blender to obtain the first extract of milk. Strain and reserve. Then put the coconut and 2 cups warm water into a blender and blend. Drain the second extract.

2 Peel and coarsely chop the ginger and garlic.

3 In a frying pan, over a low heat, put 1 tablespoon of the oil just to grease the pan and sauté the remaining coconut for 5 minutes. Remove from the heat and set aside.

4 Add another tablespoon of oil just to grease the pan and sauté the red chillies for 2–3 minutes, then add the coriander, mustard and fenugreek seeds, the cinnamon, cumin seeds, peppercorns, cloves and turmeric, in this order. Stir continuously. One minute after putting in the last item, remove from the heat.

5 Put these spices into a blender with the fried coconut, the tamarind, half the onion and ½ cup of the second coconut milk and blend to make a smooth paste. This will take at least 5 minutes.

6 Heat 3 tablespoons of the oil in a cooking pot. Sauté the remaining chopped onion until medium-brown; this will take about 15 minutes.

7 Add the spice paste together with a little water and sauté for 3 minutes, then add the chicken and sauté for a few minutes. After 5 minutes add the second extract of coconut milk and salt to taste. Add 1 cup water. Cook on a low fire, covered, until the chicken is almost done, then add the first extract of coconut milk and the curry leaves, and boil for just 1 minute.

Lamb, boiled eggs and mixed vegetables or single vegetables, like baby okra or big chunks of cauliflower together with large pieces of potato, can be prepared in the same way.

CHICKEN CHETTINAD

KOZHI VARATHA KOSAMBU (CHETTINAD)

Chettinad is the region in Southern Tamil from where the Chettiars, the trader and mercantile community of the region, originate. They have traded with South East Asia for over a thousand years. In AD 1077 the Chola King Kulottunga sent an embassy of seventy-two merchants to the Chinese court. One can see this influence in the use of star anise, a popular spice in Chinese cooking, in these curries. Chettinad cuisine is presently the rage in Madras: the first Chettinad restaurant, 'The Raintree', opened in the mid-1980s, and has been followed by several others.

Chettinad cuisine is hot. The chicken is always cut in very small pieces on the bone – about 12 pieces from a chicken. This is an ideal dish to make using chicken drumsticks. Since it is dryish, this reddish-brown dish can be eaten with a flavoured rice like lemon or tomato rice.

Serves 5

2 teaspoons poppy seeds	2 teaspoons fresh ginger, finely chopped
½lb (225g) fresh coconut	2 teaspoons garlic, finely chopped
1 teaspoon fennel seeds	½ star anise
2-in (5-cm) cinnamon stick	3 teaspoons red chilli powder
3 green cardamoms	2½lb (1.1kg) chicken, cut as preferred
4 cloves	3 medium tomatoes, finely chopped
¾ teaspoon turmeric powder	salt
¾ teaspoon garam masala *powder*	juice of ½ lime
½ cup oil	a few curry leaves
1 large onion, chopped	⅓ cup coriander leaves, chopped

1 On a griddle or in a crêpe pan, toast the poppy seeds for a few minutes until light brown. Crush with a rolling pin, then soak in a little water for 15 minutes.

2 Grind the coconut together with the poppy and fennel seeds, cinnamon, cardamom, cloves and turmeric to make a fine paste.

3 Heat the oil in a large shallow cooking pot and sauté the onion for 20 minutes until lightly coloured. Add the ginger and garlic, then 2 minutes later add the star anise and red chilli powder, followed by the spice paste and 2 tablespoons water. Sauté for 5 minutes, adding a little more water if required.

4 Add the chicken and sauté for 10 minutes. Add the tomatoes. When the chicken has absorbed the tomato juice, add 2 cups water and salt to taste and mix well. Cook, uncovered, for 45 minutes or until the chicken is tender. When almost done add the lime juice and curry leaves. Just before serving sprinkle with the coriander leaves.

CHICKEN STEW

(KERALA)

The word 'stew' has become part of the Indian culinary vocabulary. In Southern India, stew is made with coconut milk and Malabar coast spices. In Kerala in particular it is commonly eaten with *appams* or rice flour pancakes for breakfast or Sunday brunch. In Northern India, even roadside eateries serve a mild curry which they can stew.

The dish can be made milder still by reducing the green chilli. But it is really aromatic. A lady from Kerala says that she thinks the combination of *ghee* and oil imparts a special flavour. The Keralites use very tiny pieces of chicken on the bone. But you can use small boneless pieces too. On the bone, this quantity will serve 4, but boneless should suffice for 5.

Serves 4–5

1 x ¾-in (2½ x 2-cm) piece of fresh ginger (half cut into thin julienne, the other half into pieces)
1 teaspoon peppercorns
a little turmeric powder
2 onions, chopped coarsely
2–3 green chillies
2 cups fresh grated coconut
10–12 new potatoes
salt to taste
3 tablespoons oil
1 tablespoon ghee

½ teaspoon mustard seeds
1 cinnamon or bay leaf
2 garlic cloves, sliced lengthwise
2-in (5-cm) cinnamon stick
4 cardamoms
3 cloves
20 curry leaves
1¾ lb (800g) boneless, skinless chicken pieces
1 carrot, peeled and cut into ¾-in (2-cm) strips
½ cup fresh or frozen peas
¼ teaspoon garam masala *powder*

1 Pound the ginger pieces (retain the julienne strips for later), peppercorns and turmeric into a thick uneven paste.

2 Blend together the onions and green chillies. Put the grated coconut into 2 cups water and blend to make an extract. Strain and keep to one side.

3 Scrub the potatoes and half-boil them in their skins with a pinch of salt and turmeric.

4 Heat the oil and *ghee*, and when hot add the mustard seeds. When the seeds crackle, add the cinnamon or bayleaf. When the mixture turns a khaki colour add the sliced garlic, the cinnamon stick and cardamoms. After 20 seconds add the ginger paste, cloves and curry leaves, then add the chicken and sauté in the spiced oil for 2–3 minutes.

5 Salt to taste, then add the potatoes and carrot and cook, covered, for 2 minutes. Finally add the coconut milk, half a cup of water, the peas and juliennes of ginger. Sprinkle with *garam masala* powder and cook covered till the chicken is done.

CHICKEN DOPIAZA

CHICKEN WITH ONIONS (BENGAL)

Dopiaza is a popular dish in Indian restaurants outside India. *Do* means two and *piaz* means onions in Hindi, and the term describes a dish using twice the normal proportion of onions or in which onions are used twice in the cooking process. *Dopiaza* is essentially an Indian Muslim dish and Bengal has a tradition of fine Muslim cooking. The province was ruled by the Nawab of Murshidabad and Muslim Moghal governors until the British took over. And the exiled Nawabs of Oudh, as well as the family of Tipu Sultan, came to Calcutta after ceding their kingdom in the south to the British. So there has been an inflow of Muslim culinary influences.

Bengal is a region where people are particular about their food and many Bengali men cook superbly. This is Batuk Bhattacherya's recipe and is the finest *dopiaza* I have ever tasted. At home the Bhattacherya cooks the chicken dishes and his wife makes all the fish ones.

Serves 4	2-in (5-cm) cinnamon stick
	6 cardamoms
2½lb (1.25kg) small roasting chicken	1½ teaspoons peppercorns
9 medium onions	12 cloves
8 small potatoes (optional)	3 whole red chillies
3 teaspoons red chilli powder	½ teaspoon turmeric
½ cup full-fat yoghurt	2 tomatoes, chopped
½ cup oil	1 tablespoon butter
6 plump garlic cloves, finely chopped	¾ teaspoon sugar
2 cinnamon or bay leaves	1½ teaspoons garam masala powder
2 tablespoons ginger purée	salt

1 Cut the chicken into 8 pieces on the bone. Cut 3 of the onions in half. Chop 2 of the onions coarsely. Extract the juice from the remaining 4 onions by grating them and squeezing out the juice through a cheesecloth, discarding the pulp.

2 Peel the potatoes, if using. Mix the chilli powder to a paste with a little water. Whisk the yoghurt.

3 Heat the oil in a heavy pan and fry the chopped onions until light brown. Remove and drain on kitchen paper and set aside. In the same oil, fry the garlic, bay leaves and, after a couple of minutes, add the cinnamon and cardamoms. Then, 2 minutes later, add the peppercorns, cloves and whole red chillies.

4 After 30 seconds, add the ginger purée, chilli paste and turmeric and stir continuously. Add the chicken, potatoes and tomatoes, followed by the butter, yoghurt and sugar. Cook for 10–12 minutes, stirring so that the spices do not stick to the bottom of the pan and add a little water if necessary.

5 Now add the onion halves, followed by the onion juice and salt to taste. Stir for 2–3 minutes. Then transfer to a baking dish and cook in the oven, preheated to 150°C/325°F/Gas Mark 3 and cook for 20–25 minutes. When the chicken and potatoes are done, add half the fried onions and sprinkle over the garam masala powder. Sprinkle over the remaining fried onions just before serving.

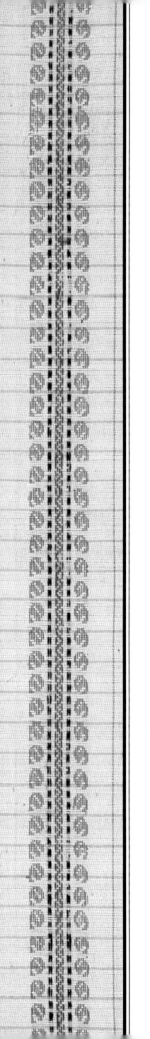

RED CHICKEN CURRY

(SYLHET, BANGLADESH)

Most of the cooks in the 'Indian' restaurants in the UK come from Bangladesh, and in particular from Sylhet. It is a pity that there are no Sylheti dishes on their menus. The food from this region is actually quite good.

A friend of mine called Barota is Bengali/Assamese and her mother comes from Sylhet. I once had this curry at her home and it was fantastic. Then I asked her to make it for me while I watched. This curry is bright red in colour because of the combination of red chilli powder (use a bright red variety) and tomato.

It is easy to make and hot and spicy. It has a thin gravy and is the right consistency to eat with rice.

Serves 4

2lb (900g) chicken pieces	12oz (350g) onions, chopped
6 plump garlic cloves	4 teaspoons Kashmiri-style chilli powder
1½ x ½-in (3 x 1-cm) piece of	3 teaspoons coriander powder
fresh ginger	½ teaspoon turmeric powder
2 large tomatoes	¾ teaspoon garam masala powder
1 tablespoon tomato paste	salt
1 teaspoon cumin seeds	1 teaspoon cider vinegar
4 tablespoons oil	

1 If there are chicken bones, use to make a stock. Strain and set aside 3 cups.

2 Purée the garlic, ginger, tomato, tomato paste and cumin seeds in a blender.

3 Heat the oil in a cooking pot and fry the onions until lightly coloured. Add the chilli powder. Count to 5, then add ¼ cup water and stir well. Bring to the boil. Then add the coriander and turmeric powders and stir continuously for a minute. Add the *garam masala* powder and sprinkle with a little water. Stir well and sauté for 1 minute.

4 Add the chicken and about 1 teaspoon salt and sauté the chicken in the spices for 5 minutes, stirring so that the spices do not stick to the pan. After 3 minutes add the tomato mixture and stir. After 2–3 minutes add 3 cups water or chicken stock and leave to cook until done. Then add the vinegar and simmer for 1 minute.

GOA PORK VINDALOO

(GOA)

Vindaloo is a dish made by descendants of, or those who lived in areas dominated by, the Portuguese. It is primarily made with chillies, *garam masala*, garlic and vinegar. The word *vindaloo* comes from a combination of *vin* for vinegar and *aloo* from *alho*, which is Portuguese for garlic. The chillies were introduced into Goa by the Portuguese, and the *garam masala* spices were those traded in the sixteenth and seventeenth centuries. This is one of the best vindaloo recipes. You can make it as hot as you want. Phil Mendes from Goa, whose recipe it is, likes her food spicy but not searing hot and therefore she de-seeds the red chillies. Vindaloo in Goa was and is traditionally made with pork. Best with boiled rice.

Serves 4

15–20 whole red chillies (preferably Kashmiri type) or	*6 plump garlic cloves*
3½ teaspoons cayenne pepper	*1 tablespoon tamarind pulp*
1 teaspoon cumin seeds	*4 teaspoons cider vinegar*
6 cloves	*⅓ cup oil*
2-in (5-cm) cinnamon stick	*3 medium onions, finely chopped*
10 peppercorns	*1½lb (700g) stewing pork, cubed*
¼ star anise	*salt*
1 teaspoon poppy seeds	*½ teaspoon* jaggery *to taste*
2 x ¼-in (5cm x 5-mm) piece of ginger	*15 curry leaves*

1 Soak the chillies in a little water to soften. Then grind all the spices, ginger, garlic and tamarind with the vinegar to make a smooth paste. Rub a little of the spice mixture on to the pork and marinate for 15 minutes.

2 Heat the oil in a cooking pot and fry the onions for about 15–20 minutes until brown. Add the spice paste and fry for a further 5 minutes, stirring continuously and adding 2 tablespoons water if necessary.

3 Add the pork and sauté in the spice mixture for 5 minutes. Add 4 cups water and salt to taste and cook over a low heat until tender. Stir in the curry leaves and simmer for 3–4 minutes; the *vindaloo* is now ready to serve.

The vinegar and oil in the dish act as preservatives and it freezes extremely well. It can also keep in the refrigerator for 2 days and will in fact be better the day after cooking.

You can also make just the spice paste in large batches and freeze it, using small amounts as and when required.

This dish is equally good using lamb or beef.

GREEN FISH CURRY

RAS CHAWAL (PARSEE STYLE)

The Parsees make various kinds of fish curry: a yellow one, a red one which has a large number of ingredients, and this green one known as *Ras Chawal* which is also made with chicken. It is quite mild with a nice herbal taste and aroma. It can be eaten with yellow rice, or just with side vegetables as in Western cuisine. If you wish, you can add a little fresh dill to the herb mixture.

Serves 2

4 teaspoons lime juice
a pinch of turmeric powder
salt
10–12oz (300–350g) fish fillets or steaks
2oz (50g) coconut, grated
4–5 green chillies
1 onion, chopped
1 tablespoon poppy seeds
3 garlic cloves
1oz (25g) cashew nuts

3 green cardamoms
¼ blade of mace or ¼ teaspoon mace powder
¼ teaspoon fennel seeds
1½ cups coriander leaves and stalks
a few mint leaves
1 teaspoon coriander powder
⅓ cup oil
1 teaspoon cumin seeds
1 teaspoon sugar

1 Mix half the lime juice with the turmeric, a pinch of salt and a little water and spread over the pieces of fish. Leave to marinate for 20 minutes.

2 Pound the poppy seeds in a mortar and pestle with a little water. In a blender, grind together the coconut, chillies, onion, poppy seeds, garlic, cashew nuts, cardamoms, mace and fennel.

3 Separately purée the coriander leaves and mint.

4 Mix the coriander powder with a little water to make a paste.

5 Heat the oil with the cumin seeds in a wide pan. When the cumin seeds begin to fry, add the coriander powder paste. After 10 seconds add the coconut and spice paste and sauté for 7 minutes, stirring continuously, scraping off any film that forms at the bottom of the pan.

6 Add the puréed coriander leaves and salt to taste and stir. Add the sugar and remaining lime juice. Add 1½ cups water and bring to the boil. Add the fish pieces and cook until done, about 7–10 minutes over a low to medium heat, depending on cut and size.

If the fish is to be eaten by itself or just with side vegetables without any rice, add ¾ cups water only.

You can substitute cream of coconut or coconut milk for the grated coconut. Grind the spices and cashew nuts together, and add ¾ cup coconut cream or milk with ¾ cup water after adding the fresh coriander leaves mixture.

You can use this recipe to make a mixed vegetable curry using 9oz (250g) diced vegetables, in which case add 2 cups water at the end and cook the vegetables until done.

PRAWNS IN SWEET AND HOT CURRY

PRAWN PATIA (DAHANU, NEAR BOMBAY)

The Parsees fled from Persia about 1300 years ago and settled on the Coast of Gujarat in India. Others who in recent centuries gradually arrived from Persia formed a small but distinct community in Bombay and Dahanu, just to the north, where they are known as Iranis and cultivate fruit orchards of mangoes, *chicoos* (sapotas) and lychees. This *patia* recipe is an Irani one from Dahanu. The Parsees also have a version of *patia*.
A *patia* is a curry with sweet, hot and sour flavours equally balanced. Both Parsees and Iranis serve the *patia* on auspicious family occasions, along with yellow rice and lentils, calling it by its traditional name – *dhan, dar, patio*. The Irani *patia* is slightly spicier and hotter than the Parsee one. There are many chillies in this recipe but the heat is offset by the sour tamarind and the sugar.
Traditionally served with yellow rice.

Serves 2

8oz (225g) shelled, uncooked prawns	*¾ teaspoon red chilli powder*
1½ teaspoons tamarind pulp	*1 teaspoon garam masala powder*
5 green chillies, chopped	*½ teaspoon turmeric powder*
3 plump garlic cloves	*2 medium tomatoes, finely chopped*
1 teaspoon cumin seeds	*1 teaspoon jaggery*
¼ cup oil	*10 curry leaves*
2 large onions, finely chopped	*¼ cup coriander leaves*
½ teaspoon cumin powder	*salt*
¾ teaspoon coriander powder	

1 If using fresh prawns, wash and remove the veins.

2 Soak the tamarind in ½ cup water for about 30 minutes.

3 Grind the 5 green chillies, 2 garlic cloves and cumin seeds to a paste.

4 Heat the oil in a cooking pot and fry the onions until deep pink. Add the ground paste and fry for 2 minutes, stirring well. Then add the chopped garlic and green chilli paste and fry for a further 2 minutes.

5 Add the cumin, coriander, red chilli, *garam masala* and turmeric powders. Stir constantly for 1 minute. Add the chopped tomatoes and fry for 4–5 minutes, stirring from time to time.

6 Add half the tamarind water, the *jaggery*, curry and coriander leaves and about 1½ teaspoons salt. Taste and adjust the sour, sweet and salt flavours to your taste. Add ¾ cup water and bring to the boil. Simmer for 5 minutes. Put in the prawns and cook for as long as necessary, remembering that prawns cook very quickly. This dish has a thick, non-runny gravy, and in India it is always served with a *moong dal*.

CRAB CURRY

(KONKAN COAST)

This recipe is from the home of Sunita Pitamber of Bombay, one of India's leading hostesses. The dish often graces her table. It is really hot and spicy and not for the faint-hearted. It can be made equally well with prawns or lobster. Or even with fish, in which case the chillies need to be reduced by 20 per cent, in order not to drown the flavour of the fish.

Kashmiri chillies are good because they are mild. If using a stronger variety of chilli, choose a large one with lots of skin but reduce the number depending on how hot they are. The important thing is the colour and taste of the chilli skin, not the 'heat'.

Best eaten with boiled rice.

Serves 4

1 giant crab, cut into pieces or 8 frozen crab claws
10oz (275g) coconut flesh or 1 x 14-fl oz (400-ml) tin coconut milk
1½oz (40g) whole dried Kashmiri chillies, seeds and stalks removed
½ teaspoon turmeric powder
5 garlic cloves

1½ x 1-in (4 x 2.5-cm) piece of fresh ginger
1 teaspoon poppy seeds, crushed
1 teaspoon coriander powder
1 teaspoon cumin seeds
1 onion
1oz (25g) tamarind
5 tablespoons oil
salt

1 Wash the crab well. Remove the feathery toes and the stomach sac attached to the shell just below the mouth. Take out the brown meat from the shell along with any whitish bits attached to it. Wash the main body shell to use in the curry for adding flavour. The main meat is in the claws and is white in colour.

2 Cut the coconut into small pieces. Liquidize with 1½ cups water. Strain and set aside (this is the thick, first coconut milk). Once again liquidize the coconut with 2½ cups water (this is the second coconut milk). Again strain and set aside. If using tinned coconut milk, dilute half with 2 cups water and use this as second coconut milk.

3 Soak the chillies in a little warm water to soften them.

4 In a blender or food processor, grind the chillies, turmeric powder, garlic, ginger, poppy seeds, coriander and cumin seeds, and the onion.

5 Soak the tamarind in 1 cup warm water.

6 Heat the oil in a cooking pot and add the spice paste. Let it cook over a low heat for 15 minutes, stirring all the time. If it sticks to the pan add ¼ cup water. Then add the second coconut milk and simmer for 10 minutes over a very low heat. Add the crab claws and main shell with about 1 teaspoon salt to the curry and cook for 2 minutes. Add the tamarind water and the first coconut milk and bring to the boil immediately. Then add the brown meat with whitish attachments. Heat through and then serve.

Prawns or fish fillets may also be used in this recipe. (1lb/450g prawns or 1½lb/600g firm fish fillets will be ample.)

MADRAS FISH CURRY

(COASTAL TAMIL NADU, HOMESTYLE)

Once I was interviewing a cook in Bangalore, whose cooking had 'magic'. He came from a village near Madras and I asked him to cook for me whatever curry he would make for himself if he were at home in his village. This is what he made. It was fingerlicking good. He said the marination of the fish in a combination of vinegar and lime juice eliminates the fishy smell, and grinding the coconut without adding water improves the taste. The gravy is pungent and quite thick. It is best with boiled rice.

Serves 5–6

1¾lb (800g) fish steaks or fillets, skinned
juice of ½ lime
2 teaspoons cider vinegar
8oz (225g) fresh coconut, grated
1½ x ½-in (3.5 x 1-cm) piece of
 fresh ginger
6 plump garlic cloves
1lb (450g) tomatoes, chopped
6 teaspoons poppy seeds, crushed
1½ teaspoons tamarind pulp

⅓ cup oil
¼ teaspoon mustard seeds
12oz (350g) onions, chopped
20–30 curry leaves
1 teaspoon coriander powder
½ teaspoon turmeric powder
2 teaspoons chilli powder or paprika
salt
¾ teaspoon fenugreek seeds and ¾ teaspoon
 cumin seeds, pounded together

1 Marinate the fish with the lime juice, vinegar and a little salt for 30 minutes.

2 Put the grated coconut into a blender or food processor with the ginger, garlic, tomatoes and poppy seeds. Do not add any water, but process for 30 seconds.

3 Soak the tamarind in 1 cup water for 30 minutes. Strain and set aside.

4 Heat the oil in a shallow, broad-based cooking pot and add the mustard seeds. When they crackle add the onions and fry until lightly coloured, then add the curry leaves. When the onions turn golden-brown, add the coriander, turmeric and chilli powders. Stir-fry for 1 minute.

5 Add the coconut mixture and sauté for 3–4 minutes, stirring constantly. Then add the tamarind water, about ¾ teaspoon salt and a further 2½ cups water. Bring to the boil and simmer for 3 minutes. Now gently lay in the fish pieces in a single layer and turn the heat to low. Sprinkle with a mixture of the fenugreek and cumin seeds. Cook until the fish is done.

If the fish curry is made a few hours before it is required, the flavour will seep into the fish better.

GOA FISH CURRY

(GOA)

This is Goa's signature dish, and a particular favourite in Bombay. It is one of the best fish curries of India, and has appeal both for its taste as well as its bright orangey-red colour. This colour comes from the combination of Kashmiri-type chillies and a liberal use of turmeric, and also by virtue of the tamarind being ground and fried with the turmeric, which deepens its colour.

It is quite simple to make, but it is important to get it absolutely right by following the quantity of ingredients exactly.

The Goa curry is judged by its texture, besides its colour and taste, and the last is important. The curry should be thin and smooth in consistency and to achieve this the spices and coconut are traditionally ground several times on a grinding stone but you would have to grind it in a food processor for about 10 minutes it to be ground satin-smooth. If your processor gets overheated, wait for a few minutes for it to cool, then continue grinding.

The favourite fish in India for use in curry is the pomfret, a flat fish. You can use halibut, cod or, surprisingly, salmon which goes well in a Goa curry. It can also be made with shrimps or prawns.

Serves 4–6

1¾lb (800g) fish, cut into pieces
  either on or off the bone
juice of ½ lime
¾ teaspoon turmeric powder
salt
8 red chillies, Kashmiri-type, or ordinary
  red chillies and 1½ teaspoons paprika
4oz (100g) fresh coconut
3 teaspoons coriander seeds

2 small onions, 1 chopped, 1 finely sliced
1 teaspoon cumin seeds
1½ teaspoons chopped garlic
1½ teaspoons tamarind pulp
2 tablespoons oil
1 tomato, grated or puréed
3 green chillies, slit lengthways
a few okra (optional)

1 Marinate the fish in a mixture of the lime juice, a pinch of the turmeric powder and a pinch of salt diluted in a little water, for 30 minutes. Then rinse.

2 Soak the red chillies in 1 cup water for 15 minutes. Strain and reserve the soaking water. In a blender or food processor, grind the chillies (and paprika, if used), coconut, coriander seeds, the chopped onion, cumin seeds, the remaining turmeric powder, the garlic and 1 teaspoon tamarind pulp to make a really fine and smooth paste. Add a little of the chilli soaking water to facilitate grinding, which will take between 7 and 10 minutes for a really smooth paste. Switch off the blender once or twice so that it does not get too hot.

3 Soak the remaining ½ teaspoon of tamarind in ½ cup water for 15 minutes. Strain and reserve the soaking water.

4 Heat the oil in a wide, shallow cooking pot and fry the finely sliced onion until it is lightly coloured, this takes about 7 minutes.

5 Add the spice paste and sauté over a moderate heat for 6–7 minutes, adding a little water if necessary. The paste will become a deep orange if the chilli is good quality. When the oil begins to separate from the spices in the form of little globules on the surface of the paste, it is time to add 4 cups water. Add the tomato, green chillies, okra and salt to taste and cook for 6 minutes. Then taste and see if you wish to add the reserved tamarind water. Add the fish and cook until done. Sprinkle with coriander leaves when serving.

You can keep this curry for a day in the refrigerator.

FISH IN COCONUT MILK

FISH MOLEE (KERALA)

Fish Molee, sometimes pronounced as Fish Moilee, is basically an Anglo-Indian dish, a sort of fish stew. It is common among Anglo-Indians of Bombay, Bangalore and Kerala, in fact all along the west coast of India. The recipes of all these communities are similar, only in Kerala local spices like cardamom, cloves and peppercorns are used. This is truly a Raj dish. It is a delicate-flavoured curry, easy to make and always popular. It is served with white rice, though dill-flavoured rice would be an interesting accompaniment.
The Molee is nice to make with assorted *fruits de mer*.

Serves 5

1½lb (700g) small fish fillets	*6 cloves garlic, pounded*
¼ teaspoon turmeric powder	*1-in (2.5-cm) square piece of fresh ginger*
salt	*1 small tomato*
juice of ½ lime	*2 peppercorns*
8oz (225g) fresh coconut, grated or	*1 clove*
1 x 14 fl oz (400ml) tin coconut milk	*2 cardamoms*
3 tablespoons oil	*6–8 curry leaves (optional)*
1 large onion, chopped	*1 small tomato, grated or puréed*
6 green chillies, slit halfway	*a pinch of freshly ground pepper*

1 Marinate the fish by adding half of the turmeric, salt to taste and the lime juice to a little water, and then coating the fish on both sides. Leave for 15 minutes, then rinse off.

2 Soak the grated coconut in 1 cup water, then grind in a blender. Strain and set aside the liquid. Then add 2 cups water to the coconut in the blender and grind again. Strain the second coconut milk and reserve.

3 Heat the oil in a broad-based cooking pot and, on a low heat, sauté the onion, chillies, garlic and ginger until the onions are lightly coloured. This will take about 10 minutes. Add the tomato, peppercorns, clove, cardamoms and curry leaves. After 2 minutes add the coconut milk, the remaining turmeric and salt to taste, and cook for 10 minutes over a low heat. If using tinned then dilute 1 cup with 1 cup water.

4 Add the fish pieces, and the first coconut milk. Cook until the fish is done (about 3–5 minutes depending on the fish). Remove the whole spices before serving.

FISH IN MUSTARD GRAVY

SORSO BHAATE MAACH (BENGAL)

Mustard is the favourite spice of Bengal, where both mustard oil and mustard seeds are used in many dishes. This is the dish-célèbre of Bengali cuisine, and the preferred fish is the bony hilsa (*Tenulosa Ilisha*). The traditional recipes impart a rather strong flavour and I think the dish improves with the inclusion of tomato and a little lime juice.
You can use the fish of your choice, such as cod, halibut, turbot or monkfish. This dish is traditionally eaten with boiled rice.

Serves 4

1lb 5oz (600g) pieces of fish	2 green chillies
1¾ teaspoon salt	1 onion, coarsely chopped
2 tablespoons poppy seeds	2 teaspoons coriander powder
2 tablespoons brown mustard seeds	2 teaspoons cumin powder
1 teaspoon turmeric powder	1–1½ teaspoons red chilli powder
2oz (60g) fresh coconut, diced	5 tablespoons oil
1 x ¾-in (2½ x 2-cm) piece	3 tomatoes, puréed
of ginger	juice of ½ lime
6 garlic cloves	2 tablespoons coriander leaves

1 Wash the fish pieces thoroughly. Smear each piece with a little salt and leave for half an hour. Wash off.

2 Toast the poppy seeds for 2 minutes on a griddle on low heat. Then pound in a mortar and pestle, with a little water if necessary.

3 Grind together the crushed poppy seeds, the mustard seeds, turmeric, coconut, ginger, garlic, green chillies, onion, coriander, cumin, red chilli powder and 1¼ teaspoon salt, along with ½ cup water, to make a paste.

4 In a large frying pan heat the oil over a moderate heat and fry the spice paste for 6–7 minutes, stirring continuously and adding a little water at a time (up to ½ cup) as and when required.

5 Add the tomatoes and sauté for 3 minutes adding ⅔ tablespoon water if required. Then pour in 2 cups water and the lime juice and simmer for 5 minutes on a low heat. Salt to taste.

6 Add the fish pieces and cook until done. Sprinkle with fresh coriander leaves when serving.

If fresh coconut is unavailable, make the spice paste without it, and use coconut milk (from a tin or made from coconut powder) instead of the 2 cups water at the end.

FISH COOKED IN YOGHURT

DOI MAACH (BENGAL)

This is another popular fish curry from Bengal, which is usually made with carp. It is only in Bengal that you will find fish and yoghurt cooked together.

Serves 4

1lb 5oz (600g) pieces of fish
1½ teaspoons salt
2 tablespoons lemon juice
½ teaspoon turmeric powder
2 teaspoons mustard powder
1½ teaspoons coriander powder
¾ teaspoon cumin powder
1 teaspoon red chilli powder
2 teaspoons chopped ginger
2 teaspoons chopped garlic
5 tablespoons oil

½ teaspoon fenugreek seeds
1 green chilli, finely chopped
2-in (5-cm) cinnamon stick
5 green cardamoms
3 cloves
2 medium onions, finely sliced
1 cup whipped full-fat yoghurt
¾ teaspoon sugar
2 tomatoes, chopped
3 tablespoons sultanas or yellow seedless
   raisins (soaked in water)

1 Skin and wash the fish well. Mix ½ teaspoon salt with the lemon juice and smear over the fish. Leave for half an hour then wash off.

2 Mix all 5 spice powders, the ginger and garlic with ½ cup water to make a spice mixture.

3 In a large saucepan heat the oil and add the fenugreek seeds, chopped green chilli, cinnamon and cardamom. After 30 seconds add the cloves. After 10 seconds add the onions and fry till light brown (12–15 minutes). Add the spice mixture and cook on a low heat until most of the moisture has dried up. Then sauté the spices for a couple of minutes more, stirring continuously.

4 Add 2 tablespoons water and cook for 1 minute, then pour in 2 cups water and simmer for 10 minutes, so that the onions soften and the spices cook properly.

5 Turn the heat very low, add the whipped yoghurt and stir continuously for 3 minutes. Add the sugar, tomatoes and up to 1 cup water, depending on the gravy required, and 1 teaspoon salt and stir well. Put the fish in gently and cook for 3 minutes, uncovered, before turning the pieces over. Add sultanas after 3 minutes and cook, uncovered, until the fish is perfectly done.

MANGO AND YOGHURT CURRY

(GUJARAT)

In the mango season, which is in the summer in India, the Gujaratis eat the fruit as part of their main meal. They eat mango juice with *puris*. Then, in order not to waste the pulp around the skin and the seed, they use this to flavour a yoghurt curry and in fact boil the mango seed in it. This curry is known colloquially as *fajeta*, an odd name because it means something to be made fun of, or a joke! The seed and the inside of the mango skin is washed very thoroughly to remove every trace of the mango pulp, so as to avoid even a tiny bit of wastage, and this is the *raison d'être* of the curry.

This is a tasty curry, and the recipe is straightforward. The proper quantity of mango must be used to get the best results. The variety of mango normally used for this dish in India is the sweet, inexpensive *pairi*, but it can be made with any sweet mango, or even frozen pulp. The curry should be eaten with boiled rice or *parathas*. It can also be served as a side dish instead of a lentil *dal*. Mango curry is traditionally eaten only at lunch-time because mango is considered heavy to digest – the ginger and asafoetida aid digestion.

This curry also makes a wonderful soup.

Serves 4

3 cups sweet (fully ripe) mangoes or
   mango pulp, to make mango juice
4½ tablespoons full-fat yoghurt
3 tablespoons gram flour (besan)
¾ teaspoon ginger powder
1–2 green chillies
2 teaspoons ginger purée

a pinch of asafoetida (optional)
1 tablespoon oil
1 teaspoon cumin seeds
8 curry leaves
salt
jaggery or cane sugar (optional)

1   Soak the mangoes in water for 15 minutes. Roll each mango between both hands, pressing them in the process in order to soften them. When they feel softened, press the area around the stalk end, then make a small hole at the top of the fruit by removing the stalk end. In a large strainer set over a bowl, squeeze out the juice by pressing or rolling the mango between both hands. When all the juice is out, press the pulp in the strainer with a spoon to extract any remaining juice. The mango juice for this curry must be smooth, without any fibre.

2   Whisk the yoghurt until smooth. Whisking prevents the yoghurt from curdling while cooking.

3   Put the gram flour into a small bowl, add 1 cup water and mix to a very smooth paste without any lumps.

4   Put the mango juice, yoghurt and gram flour paste into a cooking pot and mix well, using a whisk if necessary. Strain. Add 2 further cups of water, and ginger powder and asafoetida.

5   In a herb mill, purée the chillies with the ginger and add to the mango and yoghurt mixture with about 2 teaspoons salt. Cook over a low heat for 15 minutes, stirring from time to time.

6   Heat the oil in a very small frying pan or stainless steel ladle that can be held over a very low heat. When hot, add the cumin seeds and fry for just 10 seconds, then add the curry leaves and fry for 6–7 seconds and add along with the hot oil to the curry mixture. Let this cook for a further 15 minutes, stirring from time to time.

7   Taste for salt and sweetness, and add more salt if necessary and sugar if desired. If using jaggery, break off a small piece, equivalent to a teaspoonful and add; it will soon melt into the curry.

WATERMELON CURRY

MATIRA CURRY (RAJASTHAN)

This recipe is from Rajasthan. In the summer, temperatures in this arid desert region exceed 100°F and in the old days, before foodstuffs from other regions were easily available, the Rajasthani had to rely on what was locally available. Watermelons, called *matira* in Rajasthan, were one of the few fruits available in the summer, and are used to make an interesting semi-dry curry.

The flavour should be hot, sweet and sour, hence the large amount of chilli powder – and Rajasthan chilli is pungent. You can substitute paprika, which is milder. Quite interesting to eat with rice, or as a side dish.

Serves 2
Serves 4 as a side dish

¼ large watermelon | *salt*
1½ teaspoons red chilli powder | *2 tablespoons oil*
a pinch of turmeric powder | *¼ teaspoon cumin seeds*
½ teaspoon coriander powder | *2-3 teaspoons lime or lemon juice*
1 teaspoon garlic purée | *sugar to taste (optional)*

1 Cut up the watermelon and remove the seeds. Peel off the skin and chop the flesh into 1½-in (4-cm) cubes. Take 1 cup of the chopped watermelon, blend and make juice. To the juice add the chilli, turmeric and coriander powders, garlic purée and salt, to taste.

2 Heat the oil in a wok and add the cumin seeds and within 20 seconds add the juice. Lower the heat and simmer for 5 minutes or so, so that the spices cook completely and the liquid is reduced by a third. If using sugar, add it now, then add the lime or lemon juice and cook for 1 minute.

3 Add the chopped watermelon and cook over a low heat for 3–4 minutes, gently tossing it until all the pieces are covered in the spice mixture.

MIXED DRIED FRUIT CURRY

DRY FRUIT KORMA (BOMBAY)

The Taj Mahal Hotel in Bombay has a magnificent ballroom where for several decades a lavish lunch used to be served every day, against a backdrop of a live orchestra. As life moved on from the age of leisure to one of practicality, the daily buffet lunch died a natural death in the late 1980s.

The buffet used to have a separate section for vegetarian food, both Indian and Western. Occasionally a version of this curry used to feature in it. It is one of my favourites.

I have adapted the recipe to make it more full-bodied although it is still mild. This is an ideal dish to serve from an important occasion when you want to prepare a vegetarian curry meal or as a side dish, in which case reduce the amount of water added towards the end. As a main course, serve with yellow or saffron rice.

Serves 4

4oz (100g) dried Hunza apricots
4oz (100g) almonds, blanched
3oz (75g) pistachios
4oz (100g) cashew nuts
1½ cups full-fat yoghurt
salt
½ teaspoon ground white pepper
4 tablespoons oil
1 cinnamon or bay leaf
2-in (5-cm) cinnamon stick
3 cloves
4 green cardamoms
3 medium onions, finely chopped
1 x ½-in (2.5 x 1-cm) piece of fresh
 ginger, chopped

4 garlic cloves, chopped
4 green chillies, chopped
1 teaspoon coriander powder
½ teaspoon cumin powder
1 teaspoon red chilli powder or paprika
2 tomatoes, chopped
3 tablespoons ghee
3oz (75g) walnut pieces
4oz (100g) seedless yellow raisins
¼ teaspoon garam masala *powder*
3 tablespoons single cream
a few maraschino cherries, to garnish

1 Soak the apricots in water for 1½ hours, then slit and remove the stones (if unpitted).

2 Soak the almonds and pistachios in hot water for 1 hour. Remove the skins. Reserve the soaking water for use in the curry.

3 Grind half the cashew nuts with a little water to make a paste.

4 Whisk the yoghurt, adding ¼ teaspoon salt and the white pepper.

5 Heat the oil in a frying pan with the cinnamon or bay leaf, cinnamon, cloves and cardamoms. Add the onions and fry until medium-brown. This will take about 20 minutes. Add the ginger, garlic and chillies, and sauté for 10 minutes. By now the onions should be dark brown. It is important for the taste and appearance of the dish that the onions should fry to a deep brown – almost *café au lait* colour.

6 Add the coriander powder and sauté for 3–4 minutes, then add the cumin and red chilli powders, stirring continuously. After a minute add the tomatoes and sauté for 2–3 minutes.

7 Remove from the heat and cool. Remove the cinnamon or bay leaf , put into a blender and purée. Then pour into a cooking pot. Add the whisked yoghurt, cashew paste and 2 cups water, with salt to taste, and simmer, covered, for 15 minutes.

8 Meanwhile, heat the *ghee* in a frying pan and fry the almonds, cashew nuts, walnut pieces, raisins, apricots and most of the pistachios for 6–7 minutes, reserving a few for the garnish.

9 Add the nuts and fruit mixture to the gravy and cook, covered, on low heat for 15 minutes. Sprinkle with *garam masala* powder and cook for a further 5 minutes until the nuts are tender.

10 Garnish with swirls of cream, flaked pistachios and maraschino cherries, just before serving.

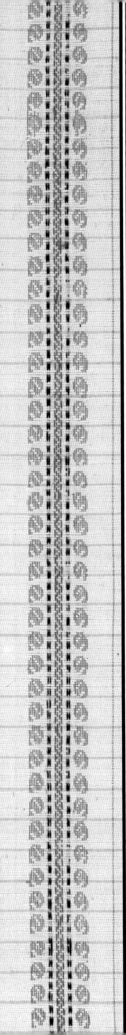

EGG CURRY

EGG KURMA (CHETTINAD)

In every part of India a curry with hardboiled eggs is made by using the most common homestyle curry recipe of the region and adding hardboiled eggs when it is ready. It is served when unexpected guests arrive as well as providing an acceptable protein curry for children.

In some parts of India, however, particularly in the Malabar and Chettinad regions, an egg curry is actually considered an important part of the cuisine. This recipe (adapted) is from the home of Mr M. A. Ramaswamy, who is the Raja of Chettinad, as shown to me by his wife, Sigapi Ramaswamy.

Serves 3

6 free range eggs, hardboiled
3 teaspoons coriander powder
1½ teaspoons chilli powder or paprika
1 teaspoon fennel seeds
1 teaspoon cumin seeds
½ teaspoon turmeric powder
½ x ¼-in (10 x 5-mm) piece of
 fresh ginger
2 plump garlic cloves

½ fresh coconut, grated or 4oz (100g)
 desiccated coconut or 1 x 7-fl oz
 (200-ml) tin of coconut milk
2 tablespoons oil
½ teaspoon fenugreek seeds
½ teaspoon fennel seeds
2-in (5-cm) cinnamon stick
8oz (225g) onions, finely chopped
8oz (225g) tomatoes, finely chopped
salt
juice of ½ lime

1 Peel the eggs and halve them lengthways.

2 Put the coriander powder, chilli powder or paprika, fennel seeds, cumin seeds, turmeric powder, ginger and garlic into a blender with 2 tablespoons water and purée to a thick paste.

3 Put the coconut into a blender with 2 cups warm water. Liquidize, then strain the coconut milk and set aside.

4 Heat the oil in a cooking pot and fry the fenugreek seeds, fennel seeds and the cinnamon for 10 seconds. Add the onion and fry until lightly coloured. Add the spice paste and sauté for 7 minutes. (It will darken in colour since it contains a lot of coriander.) Add a few drops of water if it sticks to the bottom of the pot. Then add the tomatoes and sauté for 2–3 minutes.

5 Add 3 cups warm water with salt to taste, and simmer, covered, for 20 minutes, to make a smooth gravy. Just before serving, add 2 cups of the coconut milk and bring to the boil. Add the lime juice, taste and add more salt if necessary, and gently lay in the hardboiled eggs with the yellow facing upwards. Carefully scoop into a serving dish.

You can make this curry omitting the coconut, but adding lime juice and salt, and freeze it. Then use it to make egg curry as and when you need, topping it with coconut milk at the time of reheating.

OMELETTE CURRY

(MALABAR COAST)

The Muslims and the Parsees are very fond of eggs. The Parsees have many ways of preparing them, and the Muslims of each part of India have very interesting egg dishes which are not found elsewhere. The Muslims of the Malabar Coast in Northern Kerala make a curry made with an omelette cut into broad strips. The gravy is like a thick spicy coating around the omelette strips.
Best eaten with sliced bread as an ideal dish for brunch or high tea. This recipe is from Umni Abdulla, who is an expert in the cuisine of this region.

Serves 3

For the omelette

3 free range eggs
1 small onion, finely chopped
2 green chillies, finely chopped
1 teaspoon chopped coriander leaves
a pinch of ground pepper
oil
salt

For the curry

2 tablespoons grated coconut
½ teaspoon cumin seeds
½ teaspoon fennel seeds
2 teaspoons coriander powder
½ teaspoon red chilli powder
¼ teaspoon turmeric powder
½ teaspoon garam masala *powder*
2 tablespoons oil
3 small onions, finely sliced
2–3 green chillies, chopped
2 medium tomatoes, finely chopped
1 teaspoon cider vinegar
1 tablespoon chopped coriander leaves
salt

1 Put the coconut, cumin and fennel seeds, coriander, red chilli, turmeric and *garam masala* powders into a blender with 2 tablespoons water and grind to a paste. Set aside.

2 To make the omelette, whisk the eggs. Add the onion, green chillies, coriander leaves, pepper and salt to taste and mix well.

3 Heat a little oil in a large pan and, when hot, pour in the egg and chilli mixture.

4 When the lower side of the omelette is cooked, turn the omelette over with a large spatula. Let the other side cook. Remove from the heat. First cut the omelette in half, then cut crossways into 1-in (2.5-cm) wide strips. Roll up the strips. Set aside on kitchen paper.

5 To make the curry, heat the oil in the frying pan and fry the sliced onions over a moderate heat for 10 minutes. Add the spice paste and fry for 3–4 minutes. Add a little more oil if the mixture sticks to the pan but the spices must fry properly.

6 Add the green chillies and tomatoes and sauté for 5 minutes. Then add the vinegar, 3 cups water and salt to taste. Let this curry simmer for 10 minutes.

7 Add the coriander leaves and omelette strips. Cook for 3 minutes over a very low heat, then serve.

AUBERGINE CURRY

(KERALA)

This is a homestyle curry from Kerala. The traditional way of cooking anything with tamarind is in a terracotta dish, and the terracotta in Kerala is often of the black variety. This curry is hot with a sour tang to it. Very tasty, it is best with a flavoured rice like lemon rice or dill rice, and fried South Indian *papadams*.

Serves 4

1½oz (40g) tamarind pulp
1lb (500g) baby aubergines
salt
½ fresh coconut, grated, or
   5oz (125g) frozen
6 whole red chillies
1 teaspoon coriander seeds
½ teaspoon cumin seeds
4 tablespoons oil

¼ teaspoon mustard seeds
1 teaspoon chopped garlic
1 teaspoon fresh ginger, chopped
8–10 curry leaves
14oz (400g) onions, chopped
¼ teaspoon turmeric powder
1 tablespoon chopped coriander leaves,
   to garnish

1 Soak the tamarind in ½ cup hot water for at least 30 minutes.

2 Make 2 incisions, like a cross, halfway up each aubergine. Cut off the stems. Soak in water with a pinch of salt for 15 minutes, to reduce the natural bitterness.

3 On a heated griddle toast the coconut for 5–6 minutes, then add the chillies and coriander seeds and toast for 2–3 minutes. Add the cumin and toast for 1 minute. Put into a small grinder and grind to a paste, adding a little water.

4 Heat the oil in a cooking pot and add the mustard seeds. When they crackle, add the garlic, ginger and curry leaves, then the onions and turmeric. After 25 minutes add the spice paste and sauté for a further 10–15 minutes, adding a little water if the spices stick.

5 Add 2 cups water, stir well, add salt to taste (about 1¼ teaspoons) and the aubergines and cover with the lid. After 15 minutes add the tamarind water (after squeezing the tamarind and straining it). Cook until the aubergines are tender, then remove from the heat and sprinkle with coriander leaves when serving.

SOYA KOFTA CURRY

(BOMBAY)

Processed soya beans are a relatively new item in India, gaining popular acceptance over the last decade. They have become popular with Indian housewives because they are believed to be a good source of protein, especially for vegetarians. Soya beans in packets come in two forms – granules and nuggets. Granules should be used for this dish. This recipe was devised by our cook at home, Rama, who has been with us for thirty years. Even we are surprised how he can make such a delicious dish with simple soya. For best results soak the granules in 2–3 cups water overnight. This recipe should make 20 kofta balls.

Serves 4

For the koftas

4oz (100g) soya granules (before soaking)
2oz (50g) Bengal gram (chana dal)
1 teaspoon coriander powder
¼ teaspoon cumin powder
½ teaspoon turmeric powder
½ teaspoon garam masala powder
12 peppercorns
5 green chillies
4 cloves garlic
¼ cup coriander leaves
20 mint leaves
1 egg
juice of ½ lime
1 teaspoon salt
oil for frying

For the gravy

5 tablespoons oil
2 large onions, finely chopped
¾ x ½-in (2 x 1-cm) piece of
  fresh ginger, finely chopped
2 garlic cloves, finely chopped
1 teaspoon coriander powder
¼ teaspoon turmeric powder
1 cinnamon or bay leaf
1 teaspoon red chilli powder
½ teaspoon garam masala powder
2 tomatoes, puréed
1 teaspoon salt
2 heaped teaspoons chopped
  coriander leaves

1 To make the koftas, thoroughly soak the soya and grams for at least 6 hours, overnight if possible, in 2 cups water. Then wash thoroughly and squeeze out all the water. In a fresh pan put the soya and grams into 1½ cups fresh water and bring the mixture to the boil, cooking until the grams are tender and the water totally absorbed. Add the egg and lime juice.

2 In a food processor or blender, purée the soya and grams mixture, coriander, cumin, turmeric and garam masala powders, the peppercorns, chillies, garlic, coriander and mint leaves. Season with salt to taste.

3 Shape the mixture into little balls the size of a lime.

4 Heat oil in a frying pan or wok; drop the koftas into the oil and fry until medium to dark brown. Set aside on kitchen paper.

5 To make the gravy, heat the oil in a cooking pot and fry the onions until dark brown. Add the ginger, garlic, coriander and turmeric powders with the cinnamon or bay leaf and fry for 2 minutes. Then add the red chilli and garam masala powders and fry for a few seconds, stirring continuously. Add the tomato and fry for 2 minutes. Leave to cook over a low heat for 5 minutes, adding a little water if the spices stick to the pot.

6 Now add 3 cups water and salt to taste. Bring to the boil, put in the koftas and allow to braise in the curry over a low heat for 5 minutes.

7 Sprinkle with coriander leaves, simmer for 1 minute, and then turn off the heat. Leave covered for 30 minutes to allow the koftas to absorb the curry flavour before serving.

This curry will taste even better the next day. Keep in the refrigerator. The processed soya I use in India is called Nutrela, made by Ruchi products, and it works well in this recipe.

CAULIFLOWER AND POTATO CURRY

CAULIFLOWER GASHI (MANGALORE)

In India the cauliflower is usually cooked as a dry vegetable, rarely as a curry. However on the West Coast of India, around Mangalore, the Hindu community do make a curry with it (called a *gashi*), combining it with large pieces of potato. It is actually very tasty. Serve with white rice.

Serves 2

1½ cups chopped fresh coconut
7–8 tablespoons oil
10oz (300g) onions, chopped
5 dried red chillies
2 teaspoons coriander seeds
⅛ teaspoon mustard seeds
⅛ teaspoon fenugreek seeds
¼ teaspoon cumin seeds
1-in (2½-cm) cinnamon stick
4 peppercorns
2 cloves

½ teaspoon turmeric
½ teaspoon paprika powder
1 heaped teaspoon tamarind
¾ x ½-in (2 x 1-cm) piece of ginger, finely chopped
4 garlic cloves, finely chopped
7oz (200g) potatoes, peeled and chopped into large pieces
salt, to taste
14oz (400g) cauliflower, cut into large florets

1 Soak 1 cup coconut in 2 cups warm water. Leave for half an hour then put into a blender. Strain and keep the coconut milk.

2 In a non-stick frying pan heat 1 tablespoon oil and sauté ½ cup chopped coconut for 2–3 minutes. Set aside.

3 Heat another tablespoon oil and sauté half the onions for 2–3 minutes. Set aside.

4 Heat one more tablespoon of oil and sauté the red chillies, coriander, mustard, fenugreek and cumin seeds, cinnamon, peppercorns and cloves for half a minute, and remove.

5 Now put the coconut, onions and spices into a blender. Add the turmeric, paprika and tamarind and ½ cup water and grind to a smooth paste.

6 In a saucepan, heat 4 tablespoons oil and sauté the ginger and garlic for 15 seconds, followed by the balance of the chopped onions for about 7–8 minutes, until translucent. Add the spice paste, sauté for 2 minutes, then add a little water and the potatoes and sauté for about 5 minutes. Sprinkle in the salt (about 1 teaspoon). Add ½ cup water, close the lid and cook for 6–7 minutes.

7 Now add the cauliflower, 2 cups coconut milk and cook until done.

As I suggest in the section on menus, if cooking for guests, some of whom are vegetarian, one can make extra of the spice paste for Chicken in Thick Coconut Gravy and cook this cauliflower curry for the non-meat eaters. The spice mix is very similar to the one above, but slightly less spices are used when specially making a vegetable dish like this one.

MIXED VEGETABLE CURRY

KATH KATHA (GOA)

There are hundreds of ways of making mixed vegetable curry. Almost every recipe in this book can be adapted to cook vegetables instead of lamb, chicken or fish.
This is a Hindu Goan curry. While the Goa Fish Curry (see page 120) is eaten by the Hindu and Christian of Goa alike, the Hindus alone make a vegetable curry.

Serves 4

2 onions
4 tablespoons oil
1 cup grated coconut
6 dried red chillies
2 tablespoons coriander seeds
4 cloves
10 peppercorns
2-in (5-cm) cinnamon stick
½ teaspoon mustard seeds

⅓ teaspoon cumin seeds
¼ teaspoon asafoetida (optional)
¼ teaspoon turmeric powder
1 cinnamon or bay leaf
1 blade of mace
1lb (450g) diced mixed vegetables
   (yam, carrots, potato, sweet potato, beans, peas)
salt
1 teaspoon lime or lemon juice, to taste

1 Chop 1 onion finely and slice the other.

2 Put 1 tablespoon of the oil into a non-stick frying pan, add the grated coconut and sauté for 5 minutes. Remove and set aside in a bowl.

3 Put the red chillies and coriander seeds into the same pan. After 3 minutes add the cloves, peppercorns and cinnamon and stir for 2–3 minutes. Add to the coconut in the bowl.

4 In a blender, purée the coconut, roasted spices and sliced onion, adding ½ cup water.

5 Heat the remaining oil in a cooking pot, add the mustard seeds, cumin seeds, asafoetida and turmeric powder. After a minute add the cinnamon or bay leaf and chopped onion and fry for 20–25 minutes or until the onion is browned. Add the spice mix and the mace and fry for 10–12 minutes. Pour in 3 cups water, add salt to taste and mix well.

6 Now add the vegetables in order of their cooking time. Start with yam, followed after 10 minutes by carrots and 5 minutes later by the potato and sweet potato, followed after 5 minutes by beans. Finally add the peas.

7 Cook, uncovered, over a low heat until the vegetables are tender. Then add the lime or lemon juice.

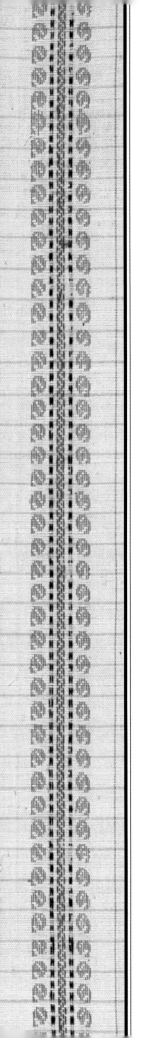

OKRA IN YOGHURT

DAHI KADHI (GUJARAT)

This curry is actually a cross between a lentil and a curry, made with yoghurt and gram flour *(besan)* as its main ingredients. It has a delightful taste and is eaten almost every day as part of the *thali* meal. Its sour-sweet flavour is tinged with a hint of chilli. It is very thin in consistency and ideal to drink as a soup.

Serves 6

2½ cups full-fat yoghurt
5 tablespoons gram flour (besan)
2 teaspoons chopped fresh ginger
1 teaspoon chopped green chilli
about 20 small okra (bhindi)
3 tablespoons sugar
salt

2 tablespoons ghee or oil
10 cloves
1½ teaspoons fenugreek seeds
1 teaspoon cumin seeds
¼ teaspoon asafoetida
about 20 curry leaves

1 Whisk the yoghurt and add the gram flour. Mix well with 4 cups water.

2 Purée the ginger and chilli together. Wash the okra and trim the stems to minimum without cutting into the vegetable.

3 Bring the yoghurt mixture to the boil in a cooking pot. Add the ginger and green chilli purée, the sugar, salt to taste (about 1 tablespoon) and okra.

4 Heat the *ghee* or oil in a ladle and fry the cloves, the fenugreek and cumin seeds, for 30 seconds, then remove from the heat and add the asafoetida. Immediately add the yoghurt mixture with the curry leaves. Cook for a total of 15–20 minutes or until the okras are tender.

Instead of okra you can use white radish cut into short pieces.

KASHMIRI-STYLE POTATO CURRY

KASHMIRI DUM ALOO (KASHMIR)

Dum means slow-cooked over a very low heat in the steam generated in a covered pot. *Aloo* means potato in Northern India and Pakistan. There are three styles of *dum aloo* – Kashmiri, Benarasi and Bengali. Each one is terrific, and different. All three, correctly prepared, are rarely found in restaurants even in India, though restaurant menus often mention *dum aloo*. The Kashmiri version is a bright red curry using the vivid red Kashmiri chilli. It can be served as a side dish to a non-vegetarian main course; one can reduce the gravy by adding less water.

Serves 6

4 Kashmiri-style dried red chillies or
  2 teaspoons paprika powder
1 cup full-fat yoghurt
1½lb (700g) potatoes
½ cup oil
8oz (225g) shallots, finely chopped
4 plump garlic cloves, finely chopped
6 green cardamoms
3-in (7.5-cm) cinnamon stick

3 cloves
2 large black cardamoms
2 teaspoons coriander powder
2½ teaspoons fennel powder
¾ teaspoon cumin powder
1¼ teaspoons ginger, finely chopped
½ teaspoon turmeric powder
2–3 tomatoes, puréed or grated
salt

1 Soak the chillies in 3 cups water for a minimum of 4 hours. With a spoon press and stir the chillies to maximize the redness of the chilli water. Strain. If using paprika, mix with 3 cups water.

2 Whisk the yoghurt and set aside.

3 Boil the potatoes in their skins for 5–6 minutes with ½ teaspoon salt. Remove from the heat and leave to cool, then peel off the skins. Pierce each potato quite deeply in several places with a toothpick. Cut each potato into quarters lengthways.

4 Heat ⅓ cup oil in a large frying pan and fry the potatoes in two batches until crispy and golden-brown; this takes about 5 minutes on a high heat. Remove from the pan. Set aside on kitchen paper.

5 In the same pan, in about 6 tablespoons oil, add the garlic, green cardamoms, cinnamon, cloves and black cardamoms and sauté for 1–2 minutes. Then add the shallots and fry till medium brown. See that they do not burn (add a little more oil if they do). Then add coriander, fennel, cumin, ginger and turmeric. Stir well.

6 After a minute add the whisked yoghurt and let this mixture fry for 2 minutes. Then add the tomato. Sauté for 2 minutes, before transferring to a cooking pot.

7 Add the chilli water, salt to taste (about 1¼ teaspoons) and the potatoes. Simmer over a very low heat until the potatoes are cooked.

Kashmiris make the same curry with turnips but you must degorge them first by rubbing with salt and leaving for at least 30 minutes. Then rinse and cook as above.

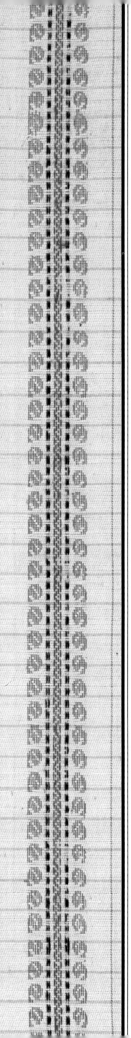

CHICKPEA CURRY

CHANAS OR CHOLE (SINDHI STYLE)

Chickpeas are known as *kabuli chanas* or *grams* from Kabul. They are popular among Punjabis who call them *chole*, and eat them with flour pancakes, *bathuras*. They are made in a sort of blackish spice mix with a dominant flavour of cumin. The Sindhis eat this curry too, but heaped on sliced bread, and the flavour has a slightly sour tang.
It can be eaten as a centrepiece with *roti*, rice or bread, or as a side dish instead of *dal*.
This recipe uses raw chickpeas but can be made very easily with chickpeas tinned in brine.
With raw chickpeas you have to start the night before by soaking them.

Serves 6 as a main course
Serves 8 as a side dish

9oz (250g) dried chickpeas
3 large onions
½oz (15g) fresh ginger
½oz (15g) garlic
9oz (250g) tomatoes, skinned
and de-seeded
2 black cardamoms
8 cloves

2 cinnamon or bay leaves
15 peppercorns
1 teaspoon cumin seeds
salt
a pinch of asafoetida
⅓ cup oil
1 teaspoon turmeric powder
½ teaspoon garam masala *powder*
1 teaspoon coriander powder
½ teaspoon ground black pepper
¾ teaspoon dried mango powder (amchur)

1 Soak the chickpeas overnight in 5 cups water (if cooking in a pressure cooker, use 4 cups).

2 Chop 2 of the onions and reserve. In a food processor, purée another onion with the ginger and garlic. Purée the tomatoes separately.

3 Placed the soaked chickpeas (and the soaking water) in a pressure cooker or ordinary cooking pot, with half the chopped onion, the black cardamoms, cloves, cinnamon or bay leaves, the peppercorns, cumin seeds, 1 teaspoon salt and asafoetida. Bring to the boil. In a pressure cooker, cook for 20 minutes and in an ordinary pot for at least 50 minutes. Drain and reserve the cooking liquid.

4 In a separate cooking pot, heat the oil. Add the reserved chopped onion and sauté for 25 minutes or until brown. Add the puréed onion, ginger and garlic mixture and sauté for 10 minutes. (If using tinned chickpeas, add now and fry with the puréed onion.)

5 Add the turmeric, *garam masala* and coriander powders, pepper and mango powder and stir thoroughly. After 1 minute add the puréed tomato and sauté for a few minutes.

6 Add the cooked chickpeas and stir gently. Add the water in which the chickpeas were cooked (you can strain away the spices since their flavour is already extracted) and cook until tender. Add salt to taste at the end of cooking.

Canned chickpeas can be used; you will need 2 x 1-lb (440-g) cans.

SINDHI CURRY

SINDHI BESAN KA CURRY (BOMBAY)

This is a curry made from just a few teaspoons of gram flour (you can substitute wholewheat flour known in India as *chapatti atta*). It is a famous dish of the Sindhi community and is usually eaten for Sunday lunch with boiled rice and fried potatoes called *took*. This curry is full of vegetables and lentils, thus an ideal dish to make for vegetarian guests, and the consistency is that of a thin *dal*.
It is also quite nice just as a soup – one can add a spoonful of boiled rice when serving it.
It is considered heavy to digest, so is always eaten at lunchtime.

Serves 6

1½ teaspoons tamarind pulp
6 cocum pieces (optional)
2–3 medium potatoes
1 small carrot
10–12 okra
6 green chillies
4 baby aubergines
5oz (150g) yam
⅓ cup oil
1 teaspoon fenugreek seeds

1 teaspoon cumin seeds
2 teaspoons fresh ginger, finely chopped
about 12 curry leaves
¼ teaspoon asafoetida
⅓ cup gram flour (or wholewheat flour)
1 teaspoon red chilli powder
1 teaspoon turmeric powder
12–15 cluster beans (gowar) or thin french beans
salt
1 heaped teaspoon sugar
8 mint leaves
1 tablespoon coriander leaves, chopped

1 Soak the tamarind in ½ cup water and, separately, the cocum, if used, in ½ cup water, each for 30 minutes.

2 Scrub the potatoes. Cut into quarters or chunks if using large potatoes. You can leave the skin on. Scrape the carrot and cut into 1½-in (4-cm) thick strips. Trim the stem from the okra but leave a stub or the okra will become mushy when cooking. Chop 2 of the green chillies. Cut the aubergines in half lengthways. Peel and cube the yam.

3 Using a cooking pot of at least 5-pint (2.8-litre) capacity, heat 4 tablespoons of the oil and add the fenugreek seeds followed by the cumin seeds. After 30 seconds add the ginger, chopped green chillies and curry leaves.

4 Fry for a minute, then add the asafoetida, gram or wholewheat flour. Stir continuously for 4–5 minutes. The flour will absorb the oil and become like a paste. But it is stirring now which will give body to the taste. Turn the heat down low and sauté properly.

5 Add the chilli and turmeric powders and another tablespoon of oil and sauté for 2–3 minutes. Then add 8 cups of hot water, stirring continuously until the paste dissolves in the water. Boil and simmer for 10 minutes.

6 Add the vegetables (the yam first, followed 10 minutes later by the potatoes and 5 minutes later by the other vegetables), with salt, sugar, 4 whole green chillies, tamarind water, cocum and cocum water. Boil until the vegetables are cooked. Then add the mint and coriander leaves. The curry will thicken slightly on cooking.

The whole green chillies are for those who like to eat chillies whole. If serving as a soup, leave out the whole chillies. This curry should be eaten with rice

RICE

Rice is the staple food of roughly half of India. It is grown typically in the delta areas and beside rivers, in irrigated areas and where the monsoons bring heavy rains. Rice supposedly originated in upper Thailand and North-East India. Fields are flooded with a few inches of water when the rice seedlings are transplanted and need to be well-watered until just before harvest. In some areas of India, only one crop per year is raised, while in areas where water is not a problem nowadays two crops per year are common. About 45 million hectares yield 80 million tonnes of rice per year. There is no part of India that does not have rice as an important feature of its cuisine. Boiled rice is eaten with curries, *dals*, yoghurt and vegetables throughout India. It is made into flour and *rotis* (griddle-made breads) are made from rice in Kerala. It is ground to make staple snack foods such as *dosas* and *idlis* all over the South. It is used to make desserts as in *mutaranjan* which are the sweet *pulaos* of the Muslims and *kheer*, a Hindu rice pudding.

Each part of India grows its own variety of rice, which is largely consumed in the region. The most popular kinds of rice, apart from Basmati, are the *jeéra* (short, fine-grain, like the cumin seed after which it is named, *jeera* meaning cumin), 'golden *sela*', (which is popular in Northern India and is parboiled Basmati rice with a golden hue, very good for making *pulaos* as the grains retain their identity), '*ambe mohue*' which has a hint of mango fragrance (*ambe* meaning mango) and is grown in Maharashtra, and *punni*, a long grain rice, which comes from Tamil Nadu. On the coast of southern India, parboiled rice is the staple food.

Basmati is the king of rice. It is famous not only for its very long, slim grain, which lengthens even further during cooking, but for its aroma. It is said that the species was originally brought from Afghanistan and planted in the hills of Dehra Dun, to the North-West of Delhi, where it benefits from the cool air at harvesting time. Now, of course, Basmati rice is grown all over the Punjab, the neighbouring state of Haryana, and in the foothills of the Himalayas, in an area known as Terai, in Uttar Pradesh. India exports Basmati rice to the UK, the US and the Middle East. It loses its aroma with too much polishing in an effort to make it extra white in colour. In the days of the Raj it was called Patna rice. Basmati rice is now cultivated in Pakistan, Thailand and the US. When buying it, be aware that all long grain rice is not Basmati rice.

It can be used for *biryanis* and on special occasions; being much more expensive than ordinary rice. To make perfect rice, the grains should be at least a year old. Many households store rice for a year, mixing a little oil into it to prevent insects. It is possible to buy older rice in markets, though the price is a bit higher. It is a pity that year-old Basmati rice is not marketed in the West.

COOKING RICE

There are two ways to do this: one is the pasta way – you boil a lot of water, a pinch of salt and a few drops of oil, add the rice and when tender pour out the excess water. In rural India this is how rice is prepared - in bulbous shaped pots with a narrow neck, to facilitate pouring off the excess water, to keep the heat in afterwards, and to slowly dry out the excess moisture.

The second way of cooking rice is the absorbtion method, in which you put exactly the amount of water required to be absorbed to give the rice a perfect consistency. It is difficult to be accurate because the exact amount of water depends on the variety of rice used, its age and so on.

Always use a pot that will be three-quarters full when the rice is cooked – and rice expands

substantially. If the rice just about fits the pot, it will be inhibited from fully fluffing up. Allow ½ cup (3½oz/100g) raw rice per person. If cooking for a party of 6–8, add an additional ½ cup in case some of your guests are indulgent.

In the Far East, electric rice cookers are used and keep the rice warm without getting it soggy. It is an effective way of cooking rice but one needs to put in the correct amount of water.

Rice is supposed to cool the body and, in the summer, it is eaten for both lunch and dinner. In the winter, colder Northern India, rice would not normally be served at night but, in the warmer South, it is eaten throughout the year. Rice is easy to digest and is given to convalescent people.

Basmati

Madras boiled rice

Amber Mohar

Golden Sela

Goan v. red rice

Colam rice

BOILED RICE FOR 2

1 cup (7oz/200g) rice
1⅓ cups water, if using basmati *(or follow packet instructions)*
salt
a few drops of oil

It is best to cook the rice about 1 hour before the start of a meal. Wash the rice twice, throw away the water, Then soak the rice for about 15–20 minutes. The rice will expand 25 per cent in this time. The exact quantity of water to be used depends on the variety of rice. For basmati, a rough guide is 1⅓ times the quantity of rice. Put the water on to boil in a large pot, add salt (about ⅙ teaspoon per cup of rice) and a few drops of oil, and when boiling add the rice and cook until 95 per cent done (around 10 minutes' boiling time for basmati). Add a little extra hot water if necessary then reduce the heat as low as possible, and remove the pot from the heat. Put a griddle, crêpe pan or skillet over the heat and put the pan on top. Cover. This will create a gentle heat and prevents the rice sticking to the bottom of the pot. Let the rice finish cooking in its own steam. When perfectly done, turn off the heat and remove the lid to allow excess moisture to evaporate. Stir gently with a fork to enable the rice to dry and give you perfectly cooked rice with separated grains.

You can season the rice with cumin seeds fried in 2 tablespoons butter, *ghee* or oil in a ladle for 30 seconds. Sprinkle over the rice when in its serving dish.

FRAGRANT RICE

When boiling rice, add ½-in (1-cm) cinnamon stick and ¼ bay leaf, together with 1 cardamom and 1 clove, if liked. Remove the spices before serving.

YELLOW RICE

This rice can be served whenever you choose as the taste and flavour do not alter, only the colour. Just add a pinch of turmeric when boiling the rice.

SAFFRON RICE

Soak a few strands of saffron in 3 tablespoons of water for 30 minutes. When the rice is done, pour the soaking water and the saffron over the cooked rice with a teaspoon and return the lid to the pot so that the aroma does not escape.

YELLOW AND WHITE RICE

BIRYANI RICE

When you eat *biryani* in restaurants you may have noticed the two-coloured, deep yellow and white rice. Well, there is a simple trick to this. Restaurateurs pour a few drops of yellow liquid food colouring randomly over the rice in the cooking pot when it is finally done. This colour then seeps down, resulting in a mixture of yellow and white rice when served. You can also add a few drops of green colouring and get three-coloured rice.

PULAO RICE

For 1 cup (7oz/200g) *pulao* rice, slice 1 small onion finely. Then heat 2 tablespoons oil in the pot in which you will cook the rice, and fry the onions until deep brown. Add the rice, a small piece of bay leaf, ½-in (1-cm) cinnamon stick and 1 clove and sauté for 2 minutes. Then cook rice as explained above under 'Boiled Rice'.

LEMON RICE

1 cup (7oz/200g) rice
8 cashew nuts
⅛ teaspoon turmeric powder
salt
3 tablespoons oil

1 green chilli, finely chopped
¼ teaspoon mustard seeds
10 curry leaves
juice of ½ lemon or 1 lime

1 Wash the rice two or three times in fresh water. Then soak for 30 minutes.

2 Meanwhile, soak the cashew nuts in 1 cup water for just 15 minutes.

3 Bring water equal to 1¼ times the volume of rice to the boil in a pot. When boiling add the rice, turmeric powder and ¼ teaspoon salt. The rice should be cooked in 11 minutes, when all the liquid should be absorbed. Turn off the heat, remove the rice and spread in a flat dish or pan to cool and dry. Leave for 30 minutes.

4 In a wok or large frying pan, heat the oil. Fry the chilli for 1 minute, then add the mustard seeds, drained cashew nuts and curry leaves and fry for 30 seconds. Add the lemon or lime juice. Add the cooked rice and stir well but carefully with a flat spatula so as not to mash the rice. The rice is now ready to serve.

FRIED BROWNED RICE

3 cups (1lb 5oz/600g) rice
5 tablespoons oil
2 medium onions, thinly sliced
½-in (1-cm) cinnamon stick
1 bay leaf

6 cloves
½ blade of mace (optional)
2 teaspoons sugar
salt

1 Soak the rice for 15 minutes. Wash well and drain.

2 Heat the oil in a pot and fry the onions until brown. Add the cinnamon, bay leaf, cloves and mace, and sauté for 5 minutes. Add the sugar and let it caramelize. Add the rice and sauté for 2 minutes. Add salt to taste (about 1 teaspoon) and 4 cups boiling water, and cook for 9–10 minutes until the rice is perfectly cooked.

DILL RICE
SOOAA CHAWAL

1 cup (7oz/200g) rice
3 tablespoons oil
2 green cardamoms

½–1 green chilli, finely chopped (optional)
⅓ cup fresh dill, finely chopped
salt

Wash and soak the rice.

Heat the oil in a cooking pot and fry the cardamoms and green chillie for 1 minute. Then add the dill and a little salt and sauté over a low heat for 2 minutes. Add the rice and sauté for 1 minute. Then add 1¼ cups hot water, if using basmati rice, or follow instructions on the packet, and cook until done.

INDIAN BREAD
OR ROTIS

The indigenous breads of India are unleavened breads known as *roti* (similar to the French word for 'roast', *rotie*), made from ground wholewheat (*aata*), millet (*bajra*) or sorghum (*jowar*). The latter two are eaten in rural Western and Central India, while wheat is the main cereal in Northern India and most of urban India except in coastal Southern and all of Eastern India where rice is the main cereal. The Muslim-influenced breads of India are leavened, like the *naans*, Khamiri *rotis* and various other kinds of *roti* breads of Bombay.

The dough is made with the ground cereal and tepid water (water described as tepid in the tropics would be slightly warm in the temperature zone). Some people add a little *ghee* or oil to the dough because it makes the *roti* softer. Some *rotis* served in restaurants, such as the *roomali roti* (thin and large like a handkerchief) have eggs mixed in the dough.

Housewives in India still largely buy their grain whole and send it to a small shop in the neighbourhood that does custom-grinding to get it ground either fortnightly or monthly. They like to make sure they get the wheat entirely whole without any adulteration. In the last few years, whole ground wheat flour in packets has made its appearance at grocers and is gaining acceptance, though there is no national popular brand.

The dough for most *rotis* is fairly standard, as follows:

> *Dough mixture*
> 1 cup wholemeal flour
> ⅓ cup warm water
> 2 teaspoons *ghee* or oil

Mix the water and flour together to make a dough, by hand or in a food processor. Then add the *ghee* or oil. Then knead it by hand for at least 5, preferably 8 minutes, as this process will make the dough slightly elastic, and the *rotis* will have a softer texture.

For best results, cover with a damp cloth and leave for 1 hour.

With this mixture you can make 12 light *chapatis* or *pooris* or 6 *parathas*. These should be enough for 3 persons.

CHAPATI

You need a griddle to make *chapatis*. In India, the *chapati* griddle is made of cast iron, is slightly concave and known as a *tawa*. Since it is used every day it does not have a chance to rust. Sprinkle a little dry flour on to a rolling board. Place the ball of dough on this and flatten. Sprinkle a little flour on top. Roll out gently to a thin pancake about 6in (15cm) in diameter. Sprinkle over a tiny amount of flour if necessary to facilitate rolling, but not too much or the *chapatis* will turn out dry. Put on to a hot griddle over a high heat. When brown spots appear, turn it over, and let it cook completely, particularly at the sides, pressing down with a spoon if necessary. Turn it over once more so that the first side which had been just slightly cooked gets completely done.

Opposite, clockwise from the top: *Naan, Chapati, Poori, Paratha*

This is the procedure for *chapatis* to be made just before the meal. Wrap them in foil or in a vacuum box (as they are now kept in India) to keep them fresh before serving.

If you want to make them several hours before the meal, brush them on both sides with a little oil when on the griddle, fold into half and wrap the whole lot in foil. Then warm in an oven just before serving.

P H U L K A

Some people prefer *chapatis* puffed up. For this you need an open flame beside the hot griddle.

Put the *chapati* on the griddle until brown spots appear, press down with the back of a large spoon, lift with a pair of tongs and hold over an open flame. When cooked turn it over on the open flame, and it will have puffed up.

Dab with a little oil, *ghee* or butter after removing from the heat. You can store the *phulkas* one on top of the other on a plate. These have to be eaten soon after making.

P O O R I S

Pooris are eaten for breakfast in Northern India along with a potato preparation. They are also eaten by Gujaratis as part of the *thali*, and quite commonly in Bengal.

Divide the *chapati* dough into 12 balls, and roll each out into a 5-in (12.5-cm) pancake, using a little wheat flour to do so.

In a deep frying pan, heat sufficient oil over a very high heat to cover the top surface of the *poori* immediately, otherwise they will not puff up, and deep-fry the *poori* individually, turning it over in the oil.

P A R A T H A S

The *paratha* is an enriched *chapati*. You can season the dough with finely chopped mint leaves and a little salt and paprika if you wish.

Divide the *chapati* dough into 6 pieces. Using a little flour, roll out each piece to an oval about 8in (20cm) long. Then draw in the sides together with your fingers to form a figure of 8, and fold to make a 4-in (10-cm) double-layered pancake. Roll out again to about 7in (17.5cm) diameter.

Put a little *ghee* or oil on a hot griddle and put on the *paratha* to cook. When one side is done, brush with a little *ghee* and turn it over. Remove when done. Stack the *parathas* one on top of another, and if not serving immediately, wrap in foil. Reheat in an oven when serving.

Parathas can be stuffed with vegetables. The most popular stuffings are boiled and spiced potato or grated and spiced radish. Spices used to season vegetables are a little red chilli, cumin powder, a pinch of dried mango powder and salt.

SIDE VEGETABLES

Although a curry is not a 'must' in an Indian meal, a vegetable dish is, both at lunch and dinner. In India a meal often consists of a vegetable dish or two, a lentil *dal*, a yoghurt dish like a *raita*, and *rotis* and/or rice. So the dishes mentioned in this section can be considered as part of such a meal, or as a side dish to a curry.

I have explained here only a few of the popular Indian vegetable dishes. They are actually quite simple to prepare.

SPINACH WITH CURD CHEESE
PALAK PANEER

Serves 2

¾ pint (450ml) milk
½ cup live yoghurt
salt
2 teaspoons lime or lemon juice
9oz (250g) fresh spinach or
   1 small packet frozen spinach

2 green chillies, chopped
½ teaspoon chopped fresh ginger
2 tablespoons oil
a pinch of fenugreek seeds
1 onion, chopped
1 garlic clove, chopped
¼ teaspoon cumin seeds
2 tomatoes, puréed

1 To make curd cheese, bring the milk just to boiling point, then add the live yoghurt with a pinch of salt and the lime or lemon juice. Continue boiling for 7–10 minutes. The milk will separate. Remove from the heat and allow to cool.

2 Place a large strainer over a bowl and pour in the milk to collect the solids in the strainer, allowing the whey to remain in the bowl below. Keep the milk solids in contact with the whey until required for cooking. When ready to use, press down the solids in the strainer with a potato masher or the back of a large spoon to squeeze the moisture out. Or use a jelly bag or cheesecloth. You will get about 4oz (100g) curd cheese or *paneer*.

3 Cook the spinach with the chillies, ginger and a pinch of salt, and just a sprinkling of water if using fresh spinach. Cook uncovered so that the bright green colour is retained. (Salt is also required for retaining the colour.) When cool, purée in a blender.

4 In a frying pan, heat the oil and fry the fenugreek seeds for 30 seconds, then add the onion and fry until lightly coloured. Add the garlic and cumin, and after 30 seconds the tomatoes. Fry for about 5 minutes.

5 When the liquid from the tomatoes has evaporated, add the curd cheese and stir gently. Add the puréed spinach and cook for a couple of minutes. It is now ready to serve.

Stir-Fried French Beans
Beans Porial

Serves 4

9oz (250g) french beans
½ teaspoon whole white urad dal
¼ cup grated coconut
¾ teaspoon cumin seeds
1½ tablespoons onion, finely chopped

10–12 curry leaves, finely chopped
salt
2 tablespoons oil or butter
1 green chilli, finely chopped and
   de seeded if liked
⅓ teaspoon mustard seeds

1   De-string and top and tail the beans. Chop into ½-in (1-cm) pieces.

2   Soak the *urad dal* in ½ cup water for 15 minutes. Drain and set aside.

3   Put the grated coconut into a bowl. Add the cumin seeds, onion and curry leaves and mix well.

4   Boil the beans in 1 cup water with ¼ teaspoon salt for 5 minutes, uncovered. The salt will help retain the bright green colour. Drain.

5   Heat the oil or butter in a frying pan and fry the chillies until pale green, then add the mustard seeds and after 20 seconds add the *urad dal* grains. After 1 minute, add the coconut and onion and sauté, stirring continuously for 2 minutes. Add the beans, toss and cook for a few minutes over a low heat until the beans are tender.

Cauliflower with Shredded Ginger
Punjabi Gobi

Cauliflower is believed to be heavy to digest and to cause wind, particularly if water is added during cooking. So in Northern India especially, cauliflower is cooked without adding any liquid. Ginger and cumin aid digestion and help to avoid flatulence. This is a very popular way of cooking cauliflower, and very tasty too.

Serves 4

1lb 2oz (500g) cauliflower
¾ teaspoon cumin seeds
3 tablespoons oil

1–2 tablespoons grated fresh ginger
a pinch of red chilli powder
¼ teaspoon cumin powder
salt
a pinch of garam masala

1   Cut the cauliflower into florets. Pound the cumin seeds.

2   Heat the oil in a wok and fry the ginger. After 30 seconds add cumin seeds, chilli and cumin powders. Then add ¼–½ teaspoon salt, stir and add the cauliflower.

3   Sprinkle with the *garam masala* powder and stir well. Cover with a lid and cook over a low heat until the cauliflower is as tender as you like it. It is now ready to serve.

Opposite, anti-clockwise from the top: *Cabbage with spices and tomato, stuffed baby aubergines, cabbage with mustard seeds, peas and carrots with cumin*

Cabbage with Spices and Tomato

Serves 4

1lb (450g) cabbage
2 medium onions
1/2 x 1/4-in (10 x 5-mm) fresh ginger
1 green chilli

2 medium tomatoes
3 tablespoons oil
1/8 teaspoon turmeric powder
1 teaspoon coriander powder
1/2 teaspoon red chilli powder
salt

1   Grate or slice the cabbage very finely and separate into shreds. Chop the onions, ginger and chilli very finely. Chop the tomatoes.

2   Heat the oil in a wok. Add the onion, ginger and chilli and sauté until the onion is browned. This takes about 25 minutes.

3   Sprinkle in the turmeric, coriander and red chilli powders. Put in the cabbage. Mix well. Cover with a lid and cook for 10 minutes, then add the tomatoes and salt and cook until done.

Stuffed Baby Aubergines
Masala Baingan

Serves 2–3

1 teaspoon coriander powder
1/4 teaspoon cumin powder
1/4 teaspoon turmeric powder
1/4 teaspoon red chilli powder

1/4 teaspoon dried mango powder
   (amchoor)
1/8 teaspoon salt
9oz (250g) baby aubergines
1 teaspoon sugar
3 tablespoons oil

1   Mix together all the spices and sugar. Make cross-slits on top of the aubergines, about 1in (2.5cm) deep. Stuff the spice mixture into the slits.

2   Heat the oil in a non-stick or thick-bottomed frying pan with a lid, and add the stuffed aubergines. Cover and cook over a low heat, turning from time to time, for about 15 minutes, until tender.

Cabbage with Mustard Seeds

Serves 2

14oz (400g) cabbage, finely shredded
salt
4 tablespoons oil

1/4 teaspoon mustard seeds
1 green chilli, chopped
1/4-in (5-mm) square piece of fresh ginger, chopped
about 10 curry leaves
1/3 teaspoon sugar

1   Soak the cabbage in water with a little salt for 15 minutes, then drain.

2   Heat the oil in a deep frying pan and add the mustard seeds. When they crackle, add the chilli, ginger and curry leaves and sauté for 1 minute. Add the cabbage, salt to taste and sugar. Sauté, mixing all the ingredients well. Cook over a low heat, uncovered, until it reaches your preferred consistency.

PEAS AND CARROTS WITH CUMIN
GAJAR MUTTER

Serves 2

3 tablespoons oil
2 medium onions, finely chopped
1 green chilli, finely chopped
1 garlic clove, finely chopped
½-in (1-cm) square piece of fresh ginger,
   finely chopped
¼ teaspoon coriander powder

1 teaspoon cumin powder
¼ teaspoon red chilli powder
½ teaspoon cumin seeds
1 small tomato, chopped
5oz (150g) (shelled weight) peas,
   fresh or frozen
3oz (75g) carrots, diced
salt

1 Heat the oil in a non-stick frying pan and over a low heat sauté the onion until brown. This will take 20–25 minutes. Then add the green chilli, garlic and ginger. Sauté for 3 minutes.

2 Add the coriander, cumin and red chilli powders, and the cumin seeds, and sauté for 2 minutes. Add 3 tablespoons water and stir well. Continue cooking the spices for 3 minutes.

3 Add the tomato and cook for a further 2–3 minutes. Then add the peas and carrots, cover and cook until tender.

OKRA WITH CHOPPED ONIONS
BHINDI PYAZ

Serves 2

9oz (250g) okra (bhindi)
salt

2 tablespoons oil
2 medium onions, chopped
1–2 green chillies
¾ teaspoon cumin seeds, crushed

1 Wash the okra and soak in a bowl of water with a pinch of salt for 5 minutes. With a sharp knife trim away the stem just above the ridge. Chop the okra into ¾-in (2-cm) pieces.

2 Heat the oil in a large, non-stick frying pan. Sauté the onions until browned. Add the chillies and fry until pale green, then add the cumin seeds and fry for 30 seconds.

3 Add the okra and salt. Stir well. Cook over a low heat, uncovered. Stir from time to time to prevent the okra sticking to the pan. Cook until done.

POTATOES

Potatoes are a very popular vegetable throughout India. They are eaten by themselves or combined with other vegetables like cauliflower, cabbage, capsicum, french beans and peas. For potatoes in a curry – the *Kashmiri Dum Aloo* recipe – see page 148.

The following recipes are all for dry potato dishes to be eaten with any curry or lentil dish.

POTATOES GUJERATI-STYLE

1lb 2oz (500g) potatoes
½ teaspoon turmeric powder
salt
2 tablespoons oil
½ teaspoon mustard seeds

½ teaspoon white, washed urad dal
16–20 curry leaves
½ teaspoon chilli powder
¼ teaspoon sugar

1 Boil the potatoes in their skins with the turmeric powder and 1 teaspoon salt. When 90 per cent done, drain, cool and peel. Cut into small pieces.

2 Heat the oil in a wok, add the mustard seeds and *urad dal*. After 10 seconds add the curry leaves and chilli powder. After 5 seconds add a little water and cook for 3 minutes, then add the sugar, and an additional seasoning of a little salt.

3 Toss the potatoes in this mixture and cook for a few minutes until they are done and heated through and have absorbed some of the oil.

POTATOES WITH FENUGREEK LEAVES
ALOO METHI (PUNJAB AND SINDH)

9oz (250g) potatoes, preferably new
¾ cup fenugreek leaves
salt
3 tablespoons oil
2 garlic cloves, chopped

1 green chilli, chopped
⅛ teaspoon turmeric powder
4 stalks of fresh dill, chopped
1 tablespoon chopped coriander leaves

1 If not using new potatoes, peel and cut into bite-sized pieces. New potatoes can be left whole with the skins on.

2 Soak the fenugreek leaves in a bowl of water with a pinch of salt for half an hour. This will remove the slightly bitter taste. Then drain and chop.

3 Heat the oil in a large frying pan or wok. Add the garlic and chilli. After a few seconds add the fenugreek leaves and fry for 1 minute.

4 Add the potatoes, turmeric powder and salt and stir-fry for 2 minutes, then add the dill and coriander leaves.

5 Cover, turn the heat to very low and leave to cook for 15 minutes or until the potatoes are done. If necessary sprinkle just a little water.

Clockwise, from the top: *potatoes in yoghurt, fried potatoes with mixed spices, potatoes with fenugreek leaves, potatoes with peanuts, potatoes Gujerati-style*

POTATOES WITH PEANUTS

1lb (450g) potatoes
a pinch of turmeric powder
2 oz (50g) peanuts
1–2 green chillies, finely chopped

4 tablespoons ghee *or oil*
1 teaspoon cumin seeds
¼ teaspoon asafoetida (optional)
a few curry leaves

1 Boil the potatoes in their skins with the turmeric powder and salt to taste. When done, drain, plunge into cold water and peel off skins.

2 Pound the peanuts or grind coarsely. Heat the *ghee* or oil in a cooking pot. When really hot, add the cumin seeds and, when they pop, sprinkle in the asafoetida, if used, chillies and curry leaves. Add the potatoes and peanuts and a pinch of salt and stir gently so that the potatoes are properly seasoned and thoroughly hot. Cook for 2 minutes and allow to heat through, then remove and serve.

FRIED POTATOES WITH MIXED SPICES
SUKHA ALOO

1lb 2oz (500g) potatoes	½ teaspoon coriander powder
½ teaspoon turmeric powder	1 teaspoon red chilli powder
salt	½ teaspoon garam masala powder
¼ cup oil	⅓ teaspoon dried mango powder (amchur)

1 Boil the potatoes in their skins with the turmeric powder and salt to taste for 5 minutes. Drain and cool, then peel off the skins. Cut into large fat chips or smaller bite-sized pieces.

2 Put the oil into a wok (preferably non-stick) with the coriander and chilli powders. Let these spices heat up with the oil over a very low heat. As soon as the oil is hot add the potatoes, and stir well. Cover with a lid and leave to cook. Stir from time to time. This will take about 20 minutes.

3 When almost done, add the *garam masala* powder and toss a couple of times. When ready sprinkle with the mango powder and toss just once, then serve.

POTATOES IN YOGHURT
DAHIWALLA ALOO (MAHARASHTRIAN-STYLE)

1lb 2oz (500 g) potatoes	½ teaspooon turmeric powder
2 medium onions	1 teaspoon red chilli powder
2oz (50g) fresh coconut, grated	2 tablespoons full-fat yoghurt
3–4 green chillies	2 tablespoons oil
2 garlic cloves	⅛ teaspoon mustard seeds
1 x ½-in (2.5 x 1-cm) piece of fresh ginger	a few curry leaves or
1½ teaspoons coriander powder	1 tablespoon coriander leaves
1 teaspoon cumin powder	salt

1 Peel the potatoes and cut crossways into round slices about ½ in (1 cm) thick.

2 Purée the onions, coconut, green chillies, garlic, ginger, coriander, cumin, half the turmeric and the red chilli powder with 2 tablespoons water in a blender or food processor.

3 Whisk the yoghurt well with a fork and set aside.

4 Boil the potatoes with the remaining ¼ teaspoon turmeric powder and salt to taste (about 1 teaspoon). When 75 per cent done, drain and cool.

5 Heat the oil in a wok and add the mustard seeds. When they crackle put in the curry or coriander leaves, followed by the puréed spices. Fry for 8–10 minutes, stirring from time to time.

6 Add the whisked yoghurt and mix well. Now add ½ cup water, taste, and season with salt. Add the sliced potatoes and cook over a low heat until done (about 15 minutes).

LENTILS
(DALS)

Dal with rice is the national dish of India. It is also eaten with *rotis* by the highest and lowest, from North India to the South and East to West. All the amino acids absent from rice are found in *dal*, which makes the combination the perfect vegetarian protein dish. It is also easy to digest.

Different *dals* are popular in different parts of India. In the Punjab and Delhi the most popular is black *urad dal*, but it is cooked with an immense amount of butter and *ghee*, so I am omitting it from this book. Also, it is not ideal for eating with a curry meal. In the East the gram *dal* is popular: in fact it is known as Bengal gram (*chana dal*). In the Uttar Pradesh, North and Western India *moong dal* is liked. It is easy to digest and as such is given to convalescents. In Uttar Pradesh, the state in India through which most of the river Ganges runs and from where the best *dal* dishes come, the *masoor dal* is also popular and prepared very well. In the South, the most commonly eaten *dal* is the *toor dal*, also known as *arhar dal*. It is used for making *sambhar*, a dish made of ground spices, eaten daily.

These *dals* come in various forms: whole or split, in the case of *moong* with the skin on or off, washed or unwashed or oiled or un-oiled. Cooked dals can be kept in the refrigerator for 2 days.

MASOOR DAL
(UTTAR PRADESH-STYLE)

9 oz (250g) pink masoor dal	½-in (1-cm) square of fresh
5 garlic cloves	ginger, chopped
1 teaspoon tamarind pulp	2–3 green chillies, chopped
(optional)	1 teaspoon coriander powder
salt	½ teaspoon cumin powder
7 oz (200g) red pumpkin, chopped	1 teaspoon red chilli powder
1 medium onion, chopped	2 teaspoons lime juice
3 small tomatoes, chopped	1 tablespoon oil or butter

1 Wash the *dal* well and soak for 30 minutes.

2 Chop 3 garlic cloves and keep separate from the other 2, which should also be chopped.

3 Soak the tamarind, if used, in ½ cup warm water for 30 minutes.

4 Bring 7 cups water to the boil in a cooking pot. Add the *dal*, return to the boil and add 1 teaspoon salt. Also add the pumpkin, onion, tomatoes, 3 garlic cloves, ginger, green chillies and the coriander, cumin and red chilli powders. Cook for 30 minutes over a moderate heat.

5 Add the tamarind water (if used) and lime juice through a strainer. Boil for 2 minutes, then remove from the heat and whisk gently with an egg beater, until the grains are completely mashed.

6 When ready to serve, heat the oil or butter in a ladle and fry the remaining chopped garlic for 1 minute. Add to the *dal*. It is really tasty. The consistency should be like a soft porridge.

MOONG DAL
(UTTAR PRADESH-STYLE)

7oz (200g) yellow moong dal
2 large tomatoes, chopped
2 green chillies, chopped
1-in (2.5-cm) square piece of
  fresh ginger, chopped
3 plump garlic cloves, chopped

¼ teaspoon turmeric powder
1 tablespoon coriander leaves, chopped
about 8 curry leaves
1 tablespoon butter or oil
salt

1   Wash the *dal* well. Soak for 15 minutes.

2   Bring 5 cups water to the boil in a cooking pot. Add the *dal* with the tomatoes, chillies, ginger, two-thirds of the garlic and the turmeric powder. Return to the boil, then add salt to taste. Cook for 30 minutes. Remove from the heat and whisk gently with an egg beater, until the grains are completely mashed. Add coriander and curry leaves and cook for 5 minutes.

3   Heat the butter or oil in a ladle, add the remaining garlic and fry until golden. Pour into the dal, which is now ready to serve. The consistency should be like a creamy soup.

DAL OF BENGAL GRAM
CHANA DAL (IN BENGAL, CHOLAR DAL)

9 z (250g) Bengal gram (chana dal)
1 tablespoon oil or ghee
1 tablespoon raisins
salt
2 garlic cloves, chopped
½-in (1-cm) piece of fresh ginger, chopped
2 green chillies, chopped
1 cinnamon or bay leaf

½ teaspoon cumin seeds
¾ teaspoon red chilli powder
½ teaspoon turmeric powder
1 tomato, chopped
½ teaspoon sugar (optional)
a pinch of asafoetida
1 tablespoon chopped coriander leaves
extra raisins to garnish

1   Wash the *dal* well. Soak for 15–20 minutes.

2   Put half the oil or *ghee* into a ladle, hold over heat, add the raisins and fry for 1 minute. Set aside on kitchen paper. Cook the *dal* in 2½ cups water for 20 minutes until soft. Add 1 teaspoon salt. Remove from the heat and leave the *dal* in the pot.

3   Put the remaining oil or *ghee* into a small frying pan and sauté the garlic, ginger, green chillies and cinnamon or bayleaf. After 2 minutes add the cumin, red chilli and turmeric powders and stir well. Add the tomato and continue to stir for a further 2 minutes.

4   Add this mixture to the dal with the sugar, if used, and the asafoetida. Bring to the boil and cook until the grains are very soft, though they should remain semi-separate. When serving, reheat the *dal* and garnish with fresh coriander leaves and chopped raisins.

In Bengal, sugar is added. In Bangladesh no sugar is added to this dish. The asafoetida is supposed to aid digestion and prevent flatulence as Bengal gram is heavy to digest.

DRY MOONG DAL
(CHURI DAL SINDHI-STYLE)

Churi means 'separate' in Sindhi. So this *dal* has a consistency like rice, in which the *dal* grains are separate and dry when cooked.

5oz (150g) yellow moong dal

salt

a pinch of turmeric powder

¼ teaspoon coriander powder

¼ teaspoon cumin powder

¼ teaspoon red chilli powder

¼ teaspoon dry mango powder (amchur)

¼ teaspoon butter or oil

1 In a small cooking pot bring 1 cup water to the boil, and add the *dal*. Return to the boil, then add salt to taste. Cook until all the water is absorbed, then turn the heat to very low, put a griddle pan over the heat and place the pot with the *dal* on it. This gives an even, mild heat, which prevents the *dal* from sticking to the bottom of the pot. All the remaining moisture will become absorbed in about 20 minutes.

2 When ready to serve, put the hot *dal* in a serving bowl. Sprinkle evenly with the spice powders, adding them one by one. Then heat the butter or oil in a ladle, and when very hot pour over the spices. Cover the bowl with a lid for a few seconds, then remove and serve. The consistency should be that of soft rice.

Clockwise, from the top right: *dal of Bengal gram, dry moong dal, moong dal Uttar Pradesh-style, masoor dal Uttar Pradesh-style*

YOGHURT
(RAITAS)

Raitas are simple to make. Essentially the yoghurt has to be whipped or whisked. You can make it with full-fat or reduced-fat yoghurt. If making it with full-fat yoghurt, then add a little water to thin it.

Season with salt, pepper and cumin powder. Then add a little sugar if desired, especially if the yoghurt is slightly sour. This is the basic *raita* recipe. Then you can add chopped coriander leaves if you wish, and sprinkle with red chilli powder or paprika. This is done in the serving bowl because it looks attractive as well as giving a slightly pungent taste.

A favourite addition to *raitas,* especially when making *chaat* (spicy street food), is to add a few teaspoons of red or tamarind chutney on the top, which gives it a nice tang. The recipe for a red chutney which goes well with *raita* is given on page 175.

You can also add other ingredients of your choice. Chopped cucumber or potato or tomato or onion are the most popular ingredients in everyday versions. Other commonly used ingredients in *raita* are boiled white pumpkin, boiled baby aubergines, blanched strips of spinach which can also be combined with raisins or dates, and *bhoondi* – tiny balls of fried *besan* or gram flour. Sindhis and Gujaratis also add *sev,* a small string-like snack made from gram flour, which is part of Bombay Mix. So mix and match as you prefer.

Incidentally, *raitas* are very cooling, so Indians avoid them in the evenings in winter.

Clockwise from top right: *potato* raita, *spinach* raita, *tomato* raita *and cucumber* raita

CUCUMBER RAITA

1 cup full-fat yoghurt
½ cup or more cucumber, peeled and
  finely chopped
salt and pepper

⅛ teaspoon cumin powder
½ teaspoon of sugar
a pinch of paprika powder
1 teaspoon coriander leaves, finely chopped

Whisk the yoghurt. Add a little water if desired. Add the cucumber, salt, pepper, cumin powder and sugar. Mix well. Put into a serving bowl and garnish with paprika and coriander leaves.

POTATO RAITA

1 large potato
salt and pepper
1½ cups full-fat yoghurt

⅛ teaspoon cumin powder
a pinch of paprika powder
1 teaspoon chopped coriander leaves

Boil the potato in its skin with a little salt until cooked. When cool, peel and cut into small cubes. Whisk the yoghurt. Add a little water if desired. Add salt and pepper to taste and the cumin, and mix well. Add the potatoes and stir gently. Put into a serving bowl. Garnish with paprika and coriander leaves.

SPINACH RAITA

15 leaves spinach, well washed
1 cup yoghurt
salt and pepper

⅛ teaspoon cumin powder
12–15 seedless raisins or 3 dates (optional)
a pinch of paprika powder

Cut the spinach into fine strips. Boil with a pinch of salt for 3–4 minutes in 1 cup water, then drain. Whisk the yoghurt. Season with salt and pepper to taste and the cumin. Add the spinach, and raisins or dates, cut into thin strips if liked. Pour into a serving bowl and sprinkle with paprika.

TOMATO RAITA

1 cup yoghurt
salt and pepper
⅛ teaspoon cumin powder

1 large tomato, finely chopped
⅛ onion, finely chopped
1 teaspoon coriander leaves

Whisk the yoghurt, adding a little water if desired. Season with salt and pepper to taste and the cumin. Combine with the tomato and onion and pour into a serving bowl. Garnish with coriander leaves in the serving bowl.

PAPADAMS

Papadams (*papads* in India) are eaten with every *dal* and rice meal, and often with curry too. In certain parts of India, such as the South, they are an essential feature, in others optional.

Papadams are made from either lentils (of various kinds) or from a combination of lentil and rice flour. The rice flour ones are from South India, and need to be fried. The lentil ones are from Northern India and can be toasted or fried. The lentil ones are seasoned with either black pepper, or garlic and chilli, or herbs and spices. Nowadays tiny *papadams* are produced for frying, which can be served with meals or as cocktail snacks. They are colloquially known as *disco papads* in Bombay. There, anything new and likable is given the prefix *disco*!

In North India it is believed that *papads* act as fat absorbers in the body. Sindhis always follow a meal with toasted *papads* and only then drink water as they believe that drinking water without eating a *papad* may lead to a cough. To toast a lentil *papad*, heat a griddle or crêpe pan until very hot, then toast the *papad* on both sides, pressing down the edges to ensure that they do not remain raw. Toasted *papads* can be kept for a couple of hours. Alternatively you can hold *papads* directly over an open gas flame. Sometimes a little oil or butter is put on the griddle pan, and when hot the *papad* is roasted on it. Fried papads cannot be kept for long or they go soggy.

For parties and special occasions, make in this way with a little butter or oil, and garnish with a few finely chopped coriander leaves, red chilli or paprika and finely chopped desiccated coconut, tasty and attractive.

You can cook them an hour or so ahead and keep on the dining table. It is not practical to make them at home.

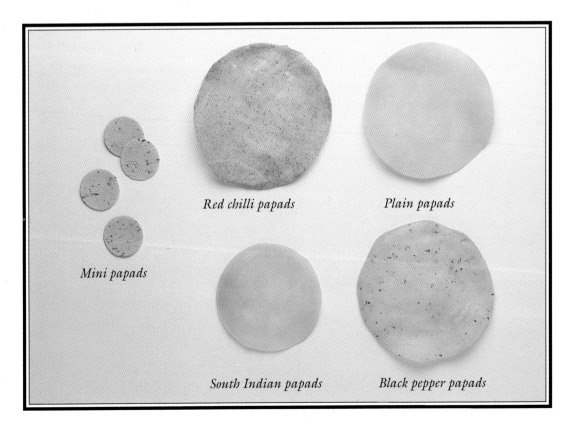

Red chilli papads

Plain papads

Mini papads

South Indian papads

Black pepper papads

CHUTNEYS

The word chutney comes from the word *chaat-na* – to lick! So chutney is something that is finger-licking good. It can be made by grinding fresh ingredients or by cooking some ingredients. Chutneys are always vegetarian, and have a sour tang: Indians like sour things and also believe that eating something sour at every meal is good for health.

Tomato chutney is made all over India. Purely herb chutneys are eaten in West and North India. Coconut chutneys are popular in Southern India and herb and coconut in Western India. Mint and yoghurt is eaten in the Punjab and Delhi side. Walnut chutney is eaten in Kashmir and groundnut chutney in Andhra Pradesh. Chutney keeps, covered in a fridge, for 2 days; thereafter the flavour deteriorates fast.

GREEN CHUTNEY WITH COCONUT

¾ cup coriander leaves
1 tablespoon mint leaves
¾ cup grated fresh coconut
2 green chillies
1 garlic clove

1 teaspoon chopped fresh ginger
½ teaspoon salt
⅓ teaspoon cumin powder
1 teaspoon caster sugar
2 teaspoons lime juice

Grind together all the ingredients except the lime juice in a blender, without adding any water. When the mixture is ground to a smooth paste, remove and put into a small serving bowl. Add the lime juice and mix well with a teaspoon. Serve with all coconut-based curries and *dhansak*.

GREEN CHUTNEY

1 cup mint leaves
1 cup coriander leaves
1 or 2 green chillies, chopped
½ small onion, chopped

¼ teaspoon cumin powder
¼ teaspoon salt
1 teaspoon sugar
2 teaspoons lime or lemon juice

Purée all the ingredients except the lime or lemon juice. Then add the juice and stir well.

RED CHUTNEY

4oz (100g) grated fresh coconut
1 small onion, chopped
2 teaspoons chopped coriander leaves
¾-in (2-cm) piece of chopped fresh ginger
1½ teaspoons red chilli powder
½ teaspoon cumin powder

2 garlic cloves
1 teaspoon sugar
3 tablespoons tomato ketchup
6 stoned dates
2 teaspoons lime juice
½ teaspoon salt

Put all the ingredients into a blender and grind to a paste.

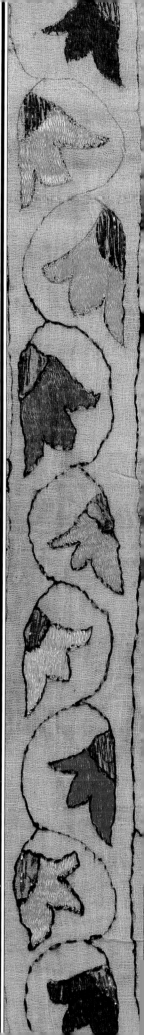

Groundnut Chutney

4oz (100g) peanuts

1 tablespoon tamarind pulp

2 green chillies

1 teaspoon salt

10 curry leaves

1 onion

1 teaspoon oil

½ teaspoon cumin seeds

½ teaspoon fenugreek seeds

½ teaspoon urad dal

2 tablespoons grated fresh coconut

1 Dry-roast the peanuts (even if they have skins) for about 15 minutes in a frying pan, with no oil. When the peanuts begin to burn, remove from the heat. Leave to cool, then remove any skins.

2 Soak the tamarind for 10 minutes in ¼ cup water. Put all the ingredients into a food-processor or blender, and grind to a paste.

Clockwise, from top right: *groundnut chutney, green chutney, green chutney with coconut*

CACHUMBERS OR RELISHES

Cachumber is to an Indian meal what *salsa* is to a Mexican one. It provides raw vegetables with a tangy touch. The most classic *cachumber* is made with raw onions, and there are many variations of this. It is finely chopped, with tomato, coriander leaves (and green chilli for those who like It) and seasoned with lime juice and salt. Variations are finely sliced onions with salt, chilli powder and lime juice.

Indians generally like to eat raw onion both for taste and for health. Onions contains sulphur, and they believe a little bit in its raw form is good. They don't worry too much about its effect on the breath; they would rinse their mouth after a meal, and chew a betel leaf or a clove or green cardamom as a breath freshener. Onions are a stimulant of passions, so Brahmin families do not eat them either cooked or raw.

In Western India, in Maharashtra and along the West coast, *cachumbers* are particularly popular and varied, and are known as *koshumbir*. They are made with all kinds of vegetables. Recipes for cabbage and carrots are given below. They are so tasty that they can be served as a salad or side vegetable. These *koshumbir* recipes have been given by Anju Sirur.

A CLASSIC ONION AND TOMATO CACHUMBER

1 medium onion
1 medium tomato
¼ green capsicum

2 teaspoons coriander leaves
lime juice
salt

Finely chop the onion, tomato, capsicum and coriander leaves. Add lime juice and a pinch of salt to taste. Mix well.

CABBAGE KOSHUMBIR

¼ cabbage
¼ fresh coconut or 2oz (50g)
* desiccated coconut*
½ mild green chilli (optional)
¼ capsicum
juice of 1 lime

½ teaspoon caster sugar
salt
2 tablespoons ghee *or oil*
a pinch of mustard seeds
8–10 curry leaves

1 Grate the cabbage finely. Grate the fresh, if used, coconut finely. Chop the lower half of the green chilli, if used, very finely. Chop the capsicum and reserve for garnishing.

2 Make a dressing with the lime juice, sugar and a pinch of salt. Mix the chopped cabbage, coconut and green chilli and pour the dressing over evenly. Mix well.

3 In a ladle heat the ghee or oil, add the mustard seeds and when they crackle add the curry leaves. Remove from the heat after 30 seconds and mix with the cabbage. Transfer to a serving dish and garnish with chopped capsicum.

SLICED ONION CACHUMBER

1 onion
⅛ teaspoon paprika

lime juice to taste
a pinch of salt

Slice the onion very finely. Season with paprika, lime juice and salt.

CARROT KOSHUMBIR

1lb (450g) carrots
2½oz (65g) desiccated fresh coconut
½ cup roasted peanuts
juice of 1 lime
½ teaspoon caster sugar

½ teaspoon salt
2 mild green chillies
2 tablespoons oil
¼ teaspoon cumin seeds

1 Grate the carrots and fresh coconut, if used, and mix together. Grind the peanuts in a coffee grinder to a very coarse consistency. Make a dressing with the lime juice, sugar and salt. Mix with the carrots.

2 Make a half-slit in the chillies, if used. Heat oil in a ladle, add the cumin seeds and after 10 seconds, add the chillies if used. After another 10 seconds pour the mixture over the carrots. Mix well, reserving the chillies as a garnish.

Clockwise from top right: *carrot koshumbir, sliced onion cachumber, classic onion and tomato cachumber and cabbage koshumbir*

178

DESSERTS

MANGO MOUSSE

Serves 6

1¾lb (800g) tinned Alphanso mango pulp
7 fl oz (200 ml) double cream
1 tablespoon powdered gelatine

2 eggs, separated
2 teaspoons caster sugar
juice of 1 lime

1 Put the mango pulp into a bowl. Beat with an electric whisk.

2 In a separate bowl, whisk the cream until it is whipped lightly.

3 Dissolve the gelatine in a little hot water.

4 Whisk the egg whites with an electric whisk until they form soft peaks. Mix the dissolved gelatine and sugar into the egg white. Add the lime juice. Fold in the whisked cream and mango. Mix well, lightly but thoroughly. Put into a large serving bowl or individual bowls and leave to set in the refrigerator for at least 3 hours.

SHRIKAND
FLAVOURED HUNG YOGHURT

This is a wonderful sweet or sour yoghurt dessert. It is so easy to make. It is served on auspicious occasions in Maharashtra.

Serves 3

1¾ pints (1 litre) yoghurt
4 teaspoons milk
½ teaspoon or less saffron
2–3 tablespoons caster sugar (to taste,
   depending on the acidity of the yoghurt)

¼ teaspoon cardamom powder
1 tablespoon ground almonds (optional)
a few slivered almonds to garnish

1 Hang the yoghurt in a piece of cheesecloth over a bowl for 3 hours and drain off the whey.

2 Put the milk and saffron into a bowl and mix vigorously with a spoon so that the flavour of the saffron blends with the milk and it becomes deep gold in colour.

3 When the yoghurt is fully drained, combine with saffron milk and add the sugar to it. Mix well to get a smooth consistency using a whisk or blender. It should have the consistency of whipped cream. Then mix in the cardamom powder and ground almonds, if used.

4 Put into a large serving bowl or individual bowls, garnish with almonds, and leave to set in the refrigerator for at least 1 hour.

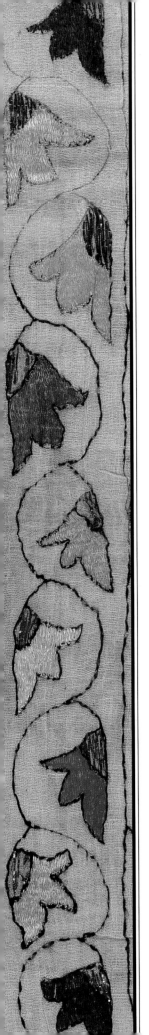

WHOLEWHEAT HALWA

ATTE KA SEERA

This dessert is relatively low in cholesterol (use a polyunsaturated oil), economical to make, and can be made in bulk and stored in a freezer. Children love it. It also makes a good addition to brunch or high tea. In India, apart from being served as a dessert, it is a winter breakfast dish. It is quite hard work to make, as you have to stir frequently for at least 20 minutes, but the result is very well worth the effort.

Serves 10

2 cups oil
3 cloves
5 cardamoms

2 cups wholewheat flour
1½ cups sugar
a little rose-water
½ cup raisins and chopped nuts, to garnish

1 Heat the oil in a heavy-based cooking pot. Put the cloves and cardamoms in to fry and as they release aromas into the oil (after 1 minute), add the flour. Stir well. Cook over a low heat for 15–20 minutes, stirring frequently until the mixture is nutty-brown.

2 Dissolve the sugar in 6 cups hot water, add to the mixture and cook for a further 7–10 minutes, stirring every now and then. It will become a sticky mixture. Remove from the heat and sprinkle in the rose-water. Serve hot, or re-heat when serving. Garnish with raisins and chopped nuts.

If kept at room temperature, excess oil will ooze out. One can remove it without affecting the taste of the dish.

KULFI

INDIAN ICE-CREAM

A favourite Indian dessert, *kulfi* (opposite) is an ice-cream traditionally made by reducing the milk as a result of boiling it for a very long time. However, it is also easy to make with evaporated milk. Traditional *kulfi* moulds are made of aluminium but are now available in plastic. Alternatively you can make the ice-cream in an ice-cube tray.

4 tablespoons sugar
3 cardamoms
2 x 1-lb (410-g) tins evaporated milk

about 12 strands of saffron
3 tablespoons double cream
2 leaves silver leaf, to decorate (optional)

1 Add the sugar and cardamoms to the milk in a heavy-based saucepan and cook over a low heat for 10 minutes, stirring and scraping the sides and bottom of the pan continuously. Remove from the heat. Remove the cardamoms and add the saffron. Mix well and leave to cool. Then stir in the cream.

2 Fill the *kulfi* moulds or pour the mixture into ice-cube trays. Freeze for 4–5 hours. Frozen *kulfi* keeps in the freezer like ice-cream.

3 To remove from the moulds, dip each into hot water and press out the *kulfi*. Decorate with silver leaf, especially for festive occasions.

SHAHI TUKRA
INDIAN BREAD PUDDING

Serves 4

4 slices white bread
1 cup ghee
3 cups of tinned evaporated milk
2½ tablespoons sugar
a few strands of saffron

a pinch of cardamom powder
2 teaspoons rose-water

To decorate
4 teaspoons pounded pistachio nuts
2 leaves silver leaf (optional)

1 Remove the crusts from the bread. Cut the slices in half diagonally. Heat half the *ghee* in a frying pan and fry the slices of bread, one at a time, for 1½ minutes or until golden-brown. Remove and keep to one side on kitchen paper.

2 Make the sauce by cooking the evaporated milk and sugar in a heavy-based saucepan for 10 minutes over a low heat. Then remove from the heat and add the saffron, cardamom powder and rose-water, mixing well.

3 To serve, place 2 slices of bread together and pour the sauce over them a short while before serving. Sprinkle with the pistachios and decorate with silver leaf.

APPLE HALWA

Carrot *halwa* or *gajar ka halwa*, as it is called in India, is a popular dessert in Indian restaurants. Apple *halwa* can be made in the same way and has an interestingly sweet–tart taste. In restaurant kitchens, a form of milk cooked until all the water has evaporated – known as *mava* or *khoya* – is used. Condensed milk is a good substitute. This *halwa* is best made with Cox's apples.

Serves 2

1½lb (700g) apples, grated
2 teaspoons sugar
juice of ½ lemon
4 tablespoons ghee *or clarified butter*
1-in (2.5-cm) cinnamon stick
3 cloves

4 tablespoons condensed milk
1 tablespoon raisins
a knob of butter
2 tablespoons calvados (optional)
almond slivers, to decorate (optional)

1 As soon as the apples are grated, sprinkle them with the sugar and lemon juice to prevent discoloration. Mix well.

2 Heat the *ghee* in a heavy-based saucepan, add the cinnamon and cloves and, after 30 seconds, the apples. Sauté for 8–10 minutes over a high heat. Add condensed milk and raisins and sauté for a further 7–8 minutes, stirring continuously and scraping the bottom and sides of the pan.

3 Glaze with the butter. This dessert should be served hot. Heat the calvados for a few seconds in a small pan and pour into the *halwa* mixture. Garnish with the almonds if using.

Opposite: *Shahi Tukra, Indian bread pudding*

GULAB JAMUNS

Serves 4

1 cup baby milk powder
3 tablespoons self-raising flour
2 tablespoons cornflour
¼ teaspoon bicarbonate of soda
12 pistachio nuts
2 cups oil for frying

For the syrup

1lb (425g) sugar
¼ lime, juice and rind
3 cardamoms
2 teaspoons rose-water or 2 drops kewra water

1 First make the syrup. Bring 2½ cups water to the boil. Add the sugar, lime juice, the rind after squeezing and only the skins of the cardamoms. Keep seeds to one side. Boil on a low heat for 20 minutes. Leave to cool. Add rose-water or kewra water for aroma. Pour the syrup into a bowl at least 4in (10cm) deep.

2 Place the milk powder, flour, cornflour and soda in a mixing bowl. Pound the cardamom seeds slightly and add. Mix well. Gradually, adding 1 tablespoon water at a time, add a total of 3–4 tablespoons water and make a dough. Try to get some air into the dough by teasing it with your hands a few times. Knead for 6–7 minutes. It will have a sticky texture. Finally put a little oil on your finger and on the dough. Roll the dough in the bowl. The bowl should now come clean. The dough should be soft, to roll into balls without cleavages. It tends to harden quickly, so get ready to fry immediately.

3 Heat the oil in a deep frying pan. First put the fire on high and after 3 minutes reduce to the lowest possible. Meanwhile divide the dough into 12 portions and roll each portion well to make balls about ¾in (2cm) diameter, and stuff each with a pistachio.

4 Deep fry the dough balls over the lowest possible heat for 5–7 minutes until they are dark brown. If they touch the hot metal of the pan they will stain and if the heat is high they will be uncooked inside. So stir constantly with a metal spoon to see that they brown evenly. The stirring spoon will also prevent the oil from becoming too hot. The balls will expand in size when frying.

5 As soon as you remove the gulab jamuns, immerse them in the cooled sugar syrup, so that they are evenly coated with syrup and cover with a lid. They will be ready to eat after half an hour. They should be eaten warm, and should be warmed in the syrup. They can be stored in the refrigerator for 5–6 days, and reheated when needed.

PLANNING A MEAL

Friends in England often ask me how an Indian housewife plans her menu. While very much part of daily life, this is a complex matter, and a number of factors have to be considered. First, as anywhere else in the world, the season and availability of produce would be taken into account. Then, depending on the time of year, heating or cooling foods would be selected, and any special family requirements taken into account. According to the Ayurveda system, some foods increase certain tendencies. For example, it might be summer and cooling foods called for, while if someone in the family has a cough, onions and rice are to be avoided.

It is important to establish whether it is full moon or new moon, for many families would not cook non-vegetarian foods on such days. Then the family or personal deity that is worshipped has its particular day of the week. So many worshippers of Shiva, the god of creation, would either fast until sundown or eat only vegetarian food on a Monday. Similarly, Tuesday is the day of the monkey-god Hanuman, symbolizing devotion and bravery. In Delhi, for example, restaurants experience a real dip in their business on Tuesdays because many people are followers of Hanuman, and since they will not eat meat, avoid going out. The planets also have their corresponding days of the week. Some family members may have, say, Saturn malefic in their horoscope at the time, in which case the family astrologer would have advised placating the planet by abstinence from particular foods – usually flesh of any kind – on Saturdays.

Once she has made her way through this maze of imponderables, the housewife gets down to the business of who is coming to dinner, what their special preferences are, and how hot or bland the dishes should be. Then she makes sure the colours of the various foods will balance, and works out how much time and help she has, and what she can afford.

In an Indian meal there is no such thing as a first course or appetizer. Appetites are automatically aroused by the wafting in of the various spicy aromas from the kitchen. All the food is placed on the table at once. The order in which it is eaten depends on the part of India in which the meal is taking place.

In an anglicized home, if only rice was being served, it would be put on the main plate, with the curry on the side or, if it has a thin gravy, in a small bowl like a compote or cereal bowl, with lentils and yoghurt in even smaller bowls. The vegetables would also be put on the side of the main plate, as would the *cachumber* and chutney. The *papadam* may be on the side plate, along with the *chapati* if it is being served. This is not as complicated as it sounds, because the amounts of each item are small, and are replenished as required. Small portions of each item are eaten with the rice or *chapati*, or in combination, as desired.

An Indian family without domestic help would eat a simple meal with rice, curry and a vegetable, with *chapatis* being made occasionally, perhaps only at weekends. They buy a lot of pitta bread, moisten it with a little water, heat it in the oven and serve it softened with a knob of butter.

The menus following are suggested for a Western audience, according to whether people like the food hot, medium or bland, and whether they prefer fish or vegetarian, and there are some suggestions for what would be appropriate for a brunch, high tea, or a buffet lunch or dinner menu.

SUGGESTED MENUS

Menus with a mild curry

1 White lamb Korma
Pulao rice (white rice flavoured with
whole spices)
Dry potatoes
Peas and carrots
Indian bread pudding (Shahi Tukra)

2 Minced lamb with coriander
Saffron rice
Cauliflower with ginger
Potatoes with peanuts
Spinach raita
Tomato chutney
Kulfi ice-cream

3 Chicken stew
White rice
French beans poryal
Potatoes with curry leaves
Mango mousse

4 Fish molée
Dill rice
Coconut and coriander chutney
Onion and tomato cachumber
Fried papadams
Gulab Jamuns

5 Mango curry (as a soup)
Soya kofta curry
Lemon or dill rice
Cabbage with mustard seeds
Potatoes with peanuts
Apple halwa

Menus with medium spicy curries

6 Kebab curry or Bhuna lamb
Saffron rice
Masoor dal
Spinach with curd cheese
Potato raita with red chutney
Wholewheat halwa (in winter)
or
Apple halwa (in summer)

7 Chicken dhansak
Pulao rice
Dry potatoes
Onion and tomato cachumber
Fried papadams
Green coconut chutney
Kulfi or ice-cream *or*
Fresh fruit

8 Prawn patia
Yellow rice
Moong dal
Okra with tomatoes
Fried papadams
Indian bread pudding

9 Chickpea curry
Yellow rice
Peas and carrots with cumin
Potatoes with yoghurt
Green coconut chutney
Shrikand